Return

to

Italy

Jacques Casanova de Seingalt

[ZHINGOORA BOOKS]

RETURN TO ITALY

GENOA—TUSCANY—ROME

CHAPTER IV

The Play—The Russian—Petri—Rosalie at the Convent

When the marquis had gone, seeing Rosalie engaged with Veronique, I set myself to translate the 'Ecossaise' for the actors at Genoa, who seemed pretty good ones, to play.

I thought Rosalie looking sad at dinner, and said,

"What is the matter, dearest? You know I do not like to see you looking melancholy."

"I am vexed at Veronique's being prettier than I."

"I see what you mean; I like that! But console your self, Veronique is nothing compared to you, in my eyes at all events. You are my only beauty; but to reassure you I will ask M. de Grimaldi to tell her mother to come and fetch her away, and to get me another maid as ugly as possible."

"Oh, no! pray do not do so; he will think I am jealous, and I wouldn't have him think so for the world."

"Well, well, smile again if you do not wish to vex me."

"I shall soon do that, if, as you assure me, she will not make me lose your love. But what made the old gentleman get me a girl like that? Do you think he did it out of mischief?"

"No, I don't think so. I am sure, on the other hand, that he wanted to let you know that you need not fear being compared with anybody. Are you pleased with her in other respects?"

"She works well, and she is very respectful. She does not speak four words without addressing me as signora, and she is careful to translate what she says from Italian into French. I hope that in a month I shall speak well enough for us to dispense with her services when we go to Florence. I have ordered Le Duc to clear out the room I have chosen for her, and I will send her her dinner from our own table. I will be kind to her, but I hope you will not make me wretched."

"I could not do so; and I do not see what there can be in common between the girl and myself."

"Then you will pardon my fears."

"The more readily as they shew your love."

"I thank you, but keep my secret."

I promised never to give a glance to Veronique, of whom I was already afraid, but I loved Rosalie and would have done anything to save her the least grief.

I set to at my translation after dinner; it was work I liked. I did not go out that day, and I spent the whole of the next morning with M. de Grimaldi.

I went to the banker Belloni and changed all my gold into gigliati sequins. I made myself known after the money was changed, and the head cashier treated me with great courtesy. I had bills on this banker for forty thousand Roman crowns, and on Lepri bills for twenty thousand.

Rosalie did not want to go to the play again, so I got her a piece of embroidery to amuse her in the evening. The theatre was a necessity for me; I always went unless it interfered with some still sweeter pleasure. I went by myself, and when I got home I found the marquis talking to my mistress. I was pleased, and after I had embraced the worthy nobleman I complimented Rosalie on having kept him till my arrival, adding gently that she should have put down her work.

"Ask him," she replied, "if he did not make me keep on. He said he would go if I didn't, so I gave in to keep him."

She then rose, stopped working, and in the course of an interesting conversation she succeeded in making the marquis promise to stay to supper, thus forestalling my intention. He was not accustomed to take anything at that hour, and ate little; but I saw he was enchanted with my treasure, and that pleased me, for I did not think I had anything to fear from a man of sixty; besides, I was glad at the opportunity of accustoming Rosalie to good society. I wanted her to be a little coquettish, as a woman never pleases in society unless she shews a desire to please.

Although the position was quite a strange one for her, she made me admire the natural aptitude of women, which may be improved or spoiled by art but which exists more or less in them all, from the throne to the milk-pail. She talked to M. de Grimaldi in a way that seemed to hint she was willing to give a little hope. As our guest did not eat, she said graciously that he must come to dinner some day that she might have an opportunity of seeing whether he really had any appetite.

When he had gone I took her on my knee, and covering her with kisses asked her where she had learnt to talk to great people so well.

"It's an easy matter," she replied. "Your eyes speak to my soul, and tell me what to do and what to say."

A professed rhetorician could not have answered more elegantly or more flatteringly.

I finished the translation; I had it copied out by Costa and took it to Rossi, the manager, who said he would put it on directly, when I told him I was going to make him a present of the play. I named the actors of my choice, and asked him to bring them to dine with me at my inn, that I might read the play and distribute the parts.

As will be guessed, my invitation was accepted, and Rosalie enjoyed dining with the actors and actresses, and especially hearing herself called Madame Casanova every moment. Veronique explained everything she did not understand.

When my actors were round me in a ring, they begged me to tell them their parts, but I would not give in on this point.

"The first thing to be done," said I, "is for you to listen attentively to the whole piece without minding about your parts. When you know the whole play I will satisfy your curiosity."

I knew that careless or idle actors often pay no attention to anything except their own parts, and thus a piece, though well played in its parts, is badly rendered as a whole.

They submitted with a tolerably good grace, which the high and mighty players of the Comedie Francaise would certainly not have done. Just as I was beginning my heading the Marquis de Grimaldi and the banker Belloni came in to call on me. I was glad for them to be present at the trial, which only lasted an hour and a quarter.

After I had heard the opinion of the actors, who by their praise of various situations shewed me that they had taken in the plot, I told Costa to distribute the parts; but no sooner was this done than the first actor and the first actress began to express their displeasure; she, because I had given her the part of Lady Alton; he, because I had not given him Murray's part; but they had to bear it as it was my will. I pleased everybody by asking them all to dinner for the day after the morrow, after dinner the piece to be rehearsed for the first time.

The banker Belloni asked me to dinner for the following day, including my lady, who excused herself with great politeness, in the invitation; and M. Grimaldi was glad to take my place at dinner at her request.

When I got to M. Belloni's, I was greatly surprised to see the impostor Ivanoff, who instead of pretending not to know me, as he ought to have done, came forward to embrace me. I stepped back and bowed, which might be put down to a feeling of respect, although my coldness and scant ceremony would have convinced any observant eye of the contrary. He was well dressed, but seemed sad, though he talked a good deal, and to some purpose, especially on politics. The conversation turned on the Court of Russia, where Elizabeth Petrovna reigned; and he said nothing, but sighed and turned away pretending to wipe the tears from his eyes. At dessert, he asked me if I had heard anything of Madame Morin, adding, as if to recall the circumstance to my memory, that we had supped together there:

"I believe she is quite well," I answered.

His servant, in yellow and red livery, waited on him at table. After dinner he contrived to tell me that he had a matter of the greatest importance he wanted to discuss with me.

"My only desire sir, is to avoid all appearance of knowing anything about you."

"One word from you will gain me a hundred thousand crowns, and you shall have half."

I turned my back on him, and saw him no more at Genoa.

When I got back to the inn I found M. de Grimaldi giving Rosalie a lesson in Italian.

"She has given me an exquisite dinner," said he, "you must be very happy with her."

In spite of his honest face, M. Grimaldi was in love with her, but I thought I had nothing to fear. Before he went she invited him to come to the rehearsal next day.

When the actors came I noticed amongst them a young man whose face I did not know, and on my enquiring Rossi told me he was the prompter.

"I won't have any prompter; send him about his business."

"We can't get on without him."

"You'll have to; I will be the prompter."

The prompter was dismissed, but the three actresses began to complain.

"If we knew our parts as well as the 'pater noster' we should be certain to come to a dead stop if the prompter isn't in his box."

"Very good," said I to the actress, who was to play Lindane, "I will occupy the box myself, but I shall see your drawers."

"You would have some difficulty in doing that," said the first actor, "she doesn't wear any."

"So much the better."

"You know nothing about it," said the actress.

These remarks put us all in high spirits, and the ministers of Thalia ended by promising that they would dispense with a prompter. I was pleased with the way the piece was read, and they said they would be letter-perfect in three days. But something happened.

On the day fixed for the rehearsal they came without the Lindane and
Murray. They were not well, but Rossi said they would not fail us eventually. I took the part of Murray, and asked Rosalie to be the Lindane.

"I don't read Italian well enough," she whispered, "and I don't wish to have the actors laughing at me; but Veronique could do it."

"Ask if she will read the part."

However, Veronique said that she could repeat it by heart.

"All the better," said I to her, laughing internally, as I thought of Soleure, for I saw that I should thus be obliged to make love to the girl to whom I had not spoken for the fortnight she had been with us. I had not even had a good look at her face. I was so afraid of Rosalie (whom I loved better every day) taking fright.

What I had feared happened. When I took Veronique's hand, and said, "Si, bella Lindana, debbe adorarvi!" everybody clapped, because I gave the words their proper expression; but glancing at Rosalie I saw a shadow on her face, and I was angry at not having controlled myself better. Nevertheless, I could not help feeling amazed at the way Veronique played the part. When I told her that I adored her she blushed up to her eyes; she could not have played the love-sick girl better.

We fixed a day for the dress-rehearsal at the theatre, and the company announced the first night a week in advance to excite public curiosity. The bills ran:

"We shall give Voltaire's Ecossaise, translated by an anonymous author: no prompter will be present."

I cannot give the reader any idea of the trouble I had to quiet Rosalie. She refused to be comforted; wept incessantly, and touched my heart by gentle reproaches.

"You love Veronique," said she, "and you only translated that piece to have an opportunity of declaring your love."

I succeeded in convincing her that she wronged me, and at last after I had lavished caresses on her she suffered herself to be calmed. Next morning she begged pardon for her jealousy, and to cure it insisted on my speaking constantly to Veronique. Her heroism went farther. She got up before me and sent me my coffee by Veronique, who was as astonished as I was.

At heart Rosalie was a great creature, capable of noble resolves, but like all women she gave way to sudden emotions. From that day she gave me no more signs of jealousy, and treated her maid with more kindness than ever. Veronique was an intelligent and well-mannered girl, and if my heart had not been already occupied she would have reigned there.

The first night of the play I took Rosalie to a box, and she would have Veronique with her. M. de Grimaldi did not leave her for a moment. The play was praised to the skies; the large theatre was full of the best people in Genoa. The actors surpassed themselves, though they had no prompter, and were loudly applauded. The piece ran five nights and was performed to full houses. Rossi, hoping perhaps that I would make him a present of another play, asked my leave to give my lady a superb pelisse of lynx-fur, which pleased her immensely.

I would have done anything to spare my sweetheart the least anxiety, and yet from my want of thought I contrived to vex her. I should never have forgiven myself if Providence had not ordained that I should be the cause of her final happiness.

"I have reason to suspect," she said one day, "that I am with child, and
I am enchanted at the thought of giving you a dear pledge of my love."

"If it comes at such a time it will be mine, and I assure you I shall love it dearly."

"And if it comes two or three weeks sooner you will not be sure that you are the parent?"

"Not quite sure; but I shall love it just as well, and look upon it as my child as well as yours."

"I am sure you must be the father. It is impossible the child can be Petri's, who only knew me once, and then very imperfectly, whilst you   and
I have lived in tender love for so long a time."

She wept hot tears.

"Calm yourself, dearest, I implore you! You are right; it cannot be Petri's child. You know I love you, and I cannot doubt that you are with child by me and by me alone. If you give me a baby as pretty as yourself, it will be mine indeed. Calm yourself."

"How can I be calm when you can have such a suspicion?"

We said no more about it; but in spite of my tenderness, my caresses, and all the trifling cares which bear witness to love, she was often sad and thoughtful. How many times I reproached myself bitterly for having let out my silly calculations.

A few days later she gave me a sealed letter, saying,—

"The servant has given me this letter when you were away. I am offended by his doing so, and I want you to avenge me."

I called the man, and said,—

"Where did you get this letter?"

"From a young man, who is unknown to me. He gave me a crown, and begged me to give the letter to the lady without your seeing me, and he promised to give me two crowns more if I brought him a reply tomorrow. I did not think I was doing wrong, sir, as the lady was at perfect liberty to tell you."

"That's all very well, but you must go, as the lady, who gave me the letter unopened, as you can see for yourself, is offended with you."

I called Le Duc, who paid the man and sent him away. I opened the letter, and found it to be from Petri. Rosalie left my side, not wishing to read the contents. The letter ran as follows:

"I have seen you, my dear Rosalie. It was just as you were coming out of the theatre, escorted by the Marquis de Grimaldi, who is my godfather. I have not deceived you; I was still intending to come and marry you at Marseilles next spring, as I promised. I love you faithfully, and if you are still my good Rosalie I am ready to marry you here in the presence of my kinfolk. If you have done wrong I promise never to speak of it, for I know that it was I who led you astray. Tell me, I entreat you, whether I may speak to the Marquis de Grimaldi with regard to you. I am ready to receive you from the hands of the gentleman with whom you are living, provided you are not his wife. Be sure, if you are still free, that you can only recover your honour by marrying your seducer."

"This letter comes from an honourable man who is worthy of Rosalie," I thought to myself, "and that's more than I shall be, unless I marry her myself. But Rosalie must decide."

I called her to me, gave her the letter, and begged her to read it attentively. She did so, and gave it me back, asking me if I advised her to accept Petri's offer.

"If you do dear Rosalie, I shall die of grief; but if I do not yield you, my honour bids me marry you, and that I am quite ready to do."

At this the charming girl threw herself on my breast, crying in the voice of true love, "I love you and you alone, darling; but it is not true that your honour bids you marry me. Ours is a marriage of the heart; our love is mutual, and that is enough for my happiness."

"Dear Rosalie, I adore you, but I am the best judge of my own honour. If Petri is a well-to-do man and a man who would make you happy, I must either give you up or take you myself."

"No, no; there is no hurry to decide. If you love me I am happy, for I love you and none other. I shall not answer the letter, and I don't want to hear anything more of Petri."

"You may be sure that I will say no more of him, but I am sure that the marquis will have a hand in it."

"I daresay, but he won't speak to me twice on the subject."

After this treaty—a more sincere one than the Powers of Europe usually make—I resolved to leave Genoa as soon as I got some letters for Florence and Rome. In the meanwhile all was peace and love between myself and Rosalie. She had not the slightest shadow of jealousy in her soul, and M. de Grimaldi was the sole witness of our happiness.

Five or six days later I went to see the marquis at his casino at St. Pierre d'Arena, and he accosted me by saying that he was happy to see me as he had an important matter he wished to discuss with me. I guessed what it would be, but begged him to explain himself. He then spoke as follows:

"A worthy merchant of the town brought his nephew, a young man   named

Petri, to see me two days ago. He told me that the young man is my

godson, and he asked me to protect him. I answered that as his godfather

I owed him my protection, and I promised to do what I could.

"He left my godson to talk it over with me, and he informed me that he knew your mistress before you did at Marseilles, that he had promised to marry her next spring, that he had seen her in my company, and that having followed us he found out that she lived with you. He was told that she was your wife, but not believing it, wrote her a letter saying that he was ready to marry her; but this letter fell into your hands, and he has had no reply to it.

"He could not make up his mind to lose a hope which made his happiness, so he resolved to ascertain, through my good offices, whether Rosalie would accept his proposition. He flatters himself that on his informing me of his prosperous condition, I can tell you that he is a likely man to make his wife happy. I told him that I knew you, and would speak to you on the matter, and afterwards inform him of the result of our interview.

"I have made enquires into his condition, and find that he has already amassed a considerable sum of money. His credit, morals, and reputation, are all excellent; besides, he is his uncle's sole heir, and the uncle passes for a man very comfortably off. And now, my dear M. Casanova, tell me what answer I am to make."

"Tell him that Rosalie is much obliged to him, and begs him to forget her. We are going away in three or four days. Rosalie loves me, and I her, and I am ready to marry her whenever she likes."

"That's plain speaking; but I should have thought a man like you would prefer freedom to a woman, however beautiful, to whom you would be bound by indissoluble ties. Will you allow me to speak to Rosalie myself about it?"

"You need not ask, my leave; speak to her, but in your own person and not as representing my opinions. I adore her, and would not have her think that I could cherish the thought of separating from her."

"If you don't want me to meddle in the matter, tell me so frankly."

"On the contrary, I wish you to see for yourself that I am not the tyrant of the woman I adore."

"I will talk to her to-night."

I did not come home till supper-time, that the marquis might say what he had to say in perfect freedom. The noble Genoese supped with us, and the conversation turned on indifferent subjects. After he had gone, my sweetheart told me what had passed between them. He had spoken to her in almost the same words that he had addressed to me, and our replies were nearly identical, though she had requested the marquis to say no more about his godson, to which request he had assented.

We thought the matter settled, and busied ourselves with preparations for our departure; but three or four days after, the marquis (who we imagined had forgotten all about his godson) came and asked us to dine with him at St. Pierre d'Arena, where Rosalie had never been.

"I want you to see my beautiful garden before you go," said M. Grimaldi to her; "it will be one more pleasant recollection of your stay for me."

We went to see him at noon the next day. He was with an elderly man and woman, to whom he introduced us. He introduced me by name, and Rosalie as a person who belonged to me.

We proceeded to walk in the garden, where the two old people got Rosalie between them, and overwhelmed her with politeness and complimentary remarks. She, who was happy and in high spirits, answered in Italian, and delighted them by her intelligence, and the grace which she gave to her mistakes in grammar.

The servants came to tell us that dinner was ready, and what was my astonishment on entering the room to see the table laid for six. I did not want much insight now to see through the marquis's trick, but it was too late. We sat down, and just then a young man came in.

"You are a little late," said the marquis; and then, without waiting for his apology, he introduced him to me as M. Petri, his godson, and nephew to his other guests, and he made him sit down at his left hand, Rosalie being on his right. I sat opposite to her, and seeing that she turned as pale as death the blood rushed to my face; I was terribly enraged. This small despot's plot seemed disgraceful to me; it was a scandalous insult to Rosalie and myself—an insult which should be washed away in blood. I was tempted to stab him at his table, but in spite of my agitation I constrained myself. What could I do? Take Rosalie's arm, and leave the room with her? I thought it over, but foreseeing the consequences I could not summon up courage.

I have never spent so terrible an hour as at that fatal dinner. Neither Rosalie nor myself ate a morsel, and the marquis who helped all the guests was discreet enough not to see that we left one course after another untouched. Throughout dinner he only spoke to Petri and his uncle, giving them opportunities for saying how large a trade they did. At dessert the marquis told the young man that he had better go and look after his affairs, and after kissing his hand he withdrew with a bow to which nobody replied.

Petri was about twenty-four, of a moderate height, with ordinary but yet good-natured and honest features; respectful in his manner, and sensible though not witty in what he said. After all was said and done, I thought him worthy of Rosalie, but I shuddered at the thought that if she became his wife she was lost to me forever. After he had gone, the marquis said he was sorry he had not known him before as he might be of use to him in his business.

"However, we will see to that in the future," said he, meaningly, "I mean to make his fortune."

At this the uncle and aunt, who no doubt knew what to say, began to laud and extol their nephew, and ended by saying that as they had no children they were delighted that Petri, who would be their heir, was to have his excellency's patronage.

"We are longing," they added, "to see the girl from Marseilles he is going to marry. We should welcome her as a beloved daughter."

Rosalie whispered to me that she could bear it no longer, and begged me to take her away. We rose, and after we had saluted the company with cold dignity we left the room. The marquis was visibly disconcerted. As he escorted us to the door he stammered out compliments, for the want of something to say, telling Rosalie that he should not have the honour of seeing her that evening, but that he hoped to call on her the next day.

When we were by ourselves we seemed to breathe again, and spoke to one another to relieve ourselves of the oppression which weighed on our minds.

Rosalie thought, as well as I, that the marquis had played us a shameful trick, and she told me I ought to write him a note, begging him not to give himself the trouble of calling on us again.

"I will find some means of vengeance," said I; "but I don't think it would be a good plan to write to him. We will hasten our preparations for leaving, and receive him to-morrow with that cold politeness which bears witness to indignation. Above all, we will not make the slightest reference to his godson."

"If Petri really loves me," said she, "I pity him. I think he is a good fellow, and I don't feel angry with him for being present at dinner, as he may possibly be unaware that leis presence was likely to give me offence. But I still shudder when I think of it: I thought I should have died when our eyes met! Throughout dinner he could not see my eyes, as I kept them nearly shut, and indeed he could hardly see me. Did he look at me while he was talking?"

"No, he only looked at me. I am as sorry for him as you are, for, as you say, he looks an honest fellow."

"Well, it's over now, and I hope I shall make a good supper. Did you notice what the aunt said? I am sure she was in the plot. She thought she would gain me over by saying she was ready to treat me like her own child. She was a decent-looking woman, too."

We made a good supper, and a pleasant night inclined us to forget the insult the marquis had put upon us. When we woke up in the morning we laughed at it. The marquis came to see us in the evening, and greeting me with an air of mingled confusion and vexation, he said that he knew he had done wrong in surprising me as he had, but that he was ready to do anything in his power by way of atonement, and to give whatever satisfaction I liked.

Rosalie did not give me time to answer. "If you really feel," said she, "that you have insulted us, that is enough; we are amply avenged. But all the same, sir, we shall be on our guard against you for the future, though that will be for a short while, as we are just leaving."

With this proud reply she made him a low bow and left the room.

When he was left alone with me M. Grimaldi addressed me as follows:

"I take a great interest in your mistress's welfare; and as I feel sure that she cannot long be happy in her present uncertain position, while I am sure that she would make my godson an excellent wife, I was determined that both of you should make his acquaintance, for Rosalie herself knows very little of him. I confess that the means I employed were dishonourable, but you will pardon the means for the sake of the excellent end I had in view. I hope you will have a pleasant journey, and that you may live for a long time in uninterrupted happiness with your charming mistress. I hope you will write to me, and always reckon on my standing your friend, and doing everything in my power for you. Before I go, I will tell you something which will give you an idea of the excellent disposition of young Petri, to whose happiness Rosalie seems essential.

"He only told me the following, after I had absolutely refused to take charge of a letter he had written to Rosalie, despairing of being able to send it any other way. After assuring me that Rosalie had loved him, and that consequently she could not have any fixed aversion for him, he added that if the fear of being with child was the reason why she would not marry him he would agree to put off the marriage till after the child was born, provided that she would agree to stay in Genoa in hiding, her presence to be unknown to all save himself. He offers to pay all the expenses of her stay. He made a remarkably wise reflection when we were talking it over.

"'If she gave birth to a child too soon after our marriage,' said he, 'both her honour and mine would suffer hurt; she might also lose the liking of my relations, and if Rosalie is to be my wife I want her to be happy in everything.'"

At this Rosalie, who had no doubt been listening at the door after the manner of her sex, burst into the room, and astonished me by the following speech:

"If M. Petri did not tell you that it was possible that I might be with child by him, he is a right honest man, but now I tell you so myself. I do not think it likely, but still it is possible. Tell him, sir, that I will remain at Genoa until the child is born, in the case of my being pregnant, of which I have no certain knowledge, or until I am quite sure that I am not with child. If I do have a child the truth will be made known. In the case of there being no doubt of M. Petri's being the parent, I am ready to marry him; but if he sees for himself that the child is not his I hope he will be reasonable enough to let me alone for the future. As to the expenses and my lodging at Genoa, tell him that he need not trouble himself about either."

I was petrified. I saw the consequence of my own imprudent words, and my heart seemed broken. The marquis asked me if this decision was given with my authority, and I replied that as my sweetheart's will was mine he might take her words for law. He went away in high glee, for he foresaw that all would go well with his plans when once he was able to exert his influence on Rosalie. The absent always fare ill.

"You want to leave me, then, Rosalie?" said I, when we were alone.

"Yes, dearest, but it will not be for long."

"I think we shall never see each other again."

"Why not, dearest? You have only to remain faithful to me. Listen to me. Your honour and my own make it imperative that I should convince Petri that I am not with child by him, and you that I am with child by you."

"I never doubted it, dear Rosalie."

"Yes, dear, you doubted it once and that is enough. Our parting will cost me many a bitter tear, but these pangs are necessary to my future happiness. I hope you will write to me, and after the child is born it will be for you to decide on how I shall rejoin you. If I am not pregnant I will rejoin you in a couple of months at latest."

"Though I may grieve at your resolve I will not oppose it, for I promised I would never cross you. I suppose you will go into a convent; and the marquis must find you a suitable one, and protect you like a father. Shall I speak to him on the subject? I will leave you as much money as you will want."

"That will not be much. As for M. de Grimaldi, he is bound in honour to procure me an asylum. I don't think it will be necessary for you to speak to him about it."

She was right, and I could not help admiring the truly astonishing tact of this girl.

In the morning I heard that the self-styled Ivanoff had made his escape an hour before the police were to arrest him at the suit of the banker, who had found out that one of the bills he had presented was forged. He had escaped on foot, leaving all his baggage behind him.

Next day the marquis came to tell Rosalie that his godson had no objection to make to her plan. He added that the young man hoped she would become his wife, whether the child proved to be his or not.

"He may hope as much as he likes," said Rosalie, with a smile.

"He also hopes that you will allow him to call on you now and then. I have spoken to my kinswoman, the mother-superior of convent. You are to have two rooms, and a very good sort of woman is to keep you company, wait on you, and nurse you when the time comes. I have paid the amount you are to pay every month for your board. Every morning I will send you a confidential man, who will see your companion and will bring me your orders. And I myself will come and see you at the grating as often as you please."

It was then my sad duty, which the laws of politeness enjoined, to thank the marquis for his trouble.

"'Tis to you, my lord," said I, "I entrust Rosalie. I am placing her, I am sure, in good hands. I will go on my way as soon as she is in the convent; I hope you will write a letter to the mother-superior for her to take."

"I will write it directly," said he.

And as Rosalie had told him before that she would pay for everything herself, he gave her a written copy of the agreement he had made.

"I have resolved," said Rosalie to the marquis, "to go into the convent to-morrow, and I shall be very glad to have a short visit from you the day after."

"I will be there," said the marquis, "and you may be sure that I will do all in my power to make your stay agreeable."

The night was a sad one for both of us. Love scarcely made a pause amidst our alternate complaints and consolations. We swore to be faithful for ever, and our oaths were sincere, as ardent lovers' oaths always are. But they are as nought unless they are sealed by destiny, and that no mortal mind may know.

Rosalie, whose eyes were red and wet with tears, spent most of the morning in packing up with Veronique, who cried too. I could not look at her, as I felt angry with myself for thinking how pretty she was. Rosalie would only take two hundred sequins, telling me that if she wanted more she could easily let me know.

She told Veronique to look after me well for the two or three days I should spend at Genoa, made me a mute curtsy, and went out with Costa to get a sedan-chair. Two hours after, a servant of the marquis's came to fetch her belongings, and I was thus left alone and full of grief till the marquis came and asked me to give him supper, advising that Veronique should be asked in to keep us company.

"That's a rare girl," said he, "you really don't know her, and you ought to know her better."

Although I was rather surprised, I did not stop to consider what the motives of the crafty Genoese might be, and I went and asked Veronique to come in. She replied politely that she would do so, adding that she knew how great an honour I did her.

I should have been the blindest of men if I had not seen that the clever marquis had succeeded in his well-laid plans, and that he had duped me as if I had been the merest freshman. Although I hoped with all my heart that I should get Rosalie back again, I had good reasons for suspecting that all the marquis's wit would be employed to seduce her, and I could not help thinking that he would succeed.

Nevertheless, in the position I was in, I could only keep my fears to myself and let him do his utmost.

He was nearly sixty, a thorough disciple of Epicurus, a heavy player, rich, eloquent, a master of state-craft, highly popular at Genoa, and well acquainted with the hearts of men, and still more so with the hearts of women. He had spent a good deal of time at Venice to be more at liberty, and to enjoy the pleasures of life at his ease. He had never married, and when asked the reason would reply that he knew too well that women would be either tyrants or slaves, and that he did not want to be a tyrant to any woman, nor to be under any woman's orders. He found some way of returning to his beloved Venice, in spite of the law forbidding any noble who has filled the office of doge to leave his native soil. Though he behaved to me in a very friendly manner he knew how to maintain an air of superiority which imposed on me. Nothing else could have given him the courage to ask me to dinner when Petri was to be present. I felt that I had been tricked, and I thought myself in duty bound to make him esteem me by my behaviour for the future. It was gratitude on his part which made him smooth the way to my conquest of Veronique, who doubtless struck him as a fit and proper person to console me for the loss of Rosalie.

I did not take any part in the conversation at supper, but the marquis drew out Veronique, and she shone. It was easy for me to see that she had more wit and knowledge of the world than Rosalie, but in my then state of mind this grieved rather than rejoiced me. M. de Grimaldi seemed sorry to see me melancholy, and forced me, as it were, to join in the conversation. As he was reproaching me in a friendly manner for my silence, Veronique said with a pleasing smile that I had a good reason to be silent after the declaration of love I had made to her, and which she had received so ill. I was astonished at this, and said that I did not remember having ever made her such a declaration; but she made me laugh in spite of myself, when she said that her name that day was Lindane.

"Ah, that's in a play," said I, "in real life the man who declares his love in words is a simpleton; 'tis with deeds the true lover shews his love."

"Very true, but your lady was frightened all the same."

"No, no, Veronique; she is very fond of you."

"I know she is; but I have seen her jealous of me."

"If so, she was quite wrong."

This dialogue, which pleased me little, fell sweetly on the marquis's ears; he told me that he was going to call on Rosalie next morning, and that if I liked to give him a supper, he would come and tell me about her in the evening. Of course I told him that he would be welcome.

After Veronique had lighted me to my room, she asked me to let my servants wait on me, as if she did so now that my lady was gone, people might talk about her.

"You are right," said I, "kindly send Le Duc to me."

Next morning I had a letter from Geneva. It came from my Epicurean syndic, who had presented M. de Voltaire with my translation of his play, with an exceedingly polite letter from me, in which I begged his pardon for having taken the liberty of travestying his fine French prose in Italian. The syndic told me plainly that M. de Voltaire had pronounced my translation to be a bad one.

My self-esteem was so wounded by this, and by his impoliteness in not answering my letter, with which he could certainly find no fault, whatever his criticism of my translation might be, that I became the sworn enemy of the great Voltaire. I have censured him in all the works I have published, thinking that in wronging him I was avenging myself, to such an extent did passion blind me.

At the present time I feel that even if my works survive, these feeble stings of mine can hurt nobody but myself. Posterity will class me amongst the Zoiluses whose own impotence made them attack this great man to whom civilization and human happiness owe so much. The only crime that can truthfully be alleged against Voltaire is his attacks on religion. If he had been a true philosopher he would never have spoken on such matters, for, even if his attacks were based on truth, religion is necessary to morality, without which there can be no happiness.

CHAPTER V

I Fall in Love With Veronique—Her Sister—Plot Against Plot—My Victory—Mutual Disappointment

I have never liked eating by myself, and thus I have never turned hermit, though I once thought of turning monk; but a monk without renouncing all the pleasures of life lives well in a kind of holy idleness. This dislike to loneliness made me give orders that the table should be laid for two, and indeed, after supping with the marquis and myself, Veronique had some right to expect as much, to say nothing of those rights which her wit and beauty gave her.

I only saw Costa, and asked him what had become of Le Duc. He said he was ill. "Then go behind the lady's chair," said I. He obeyed, but smiled as he did so. Pride is a universal failing, and though a servant's pride is the silliest of all it is often pushed to the greatest extremes.

I thought Veronique prettier than before. Her behaviour, now free and now reserved, as the occasion demanded, shewed me that she was no new hand, and that she could have played the part of a princess in the best society. Nevertheless (so strange a thing is the heart of man), I was sorry to find I liked her, and my only consolation was that her mother would come and take her away before the day was over. I had adored Rosalie, and my heart still bled at the thought of our parting.

The girl's mother came while we were still at table. She was astounded at the honour I shewed her daughter, and she overwhelmed me with thanks.

"You owe me no gratitude," said I to her; "your daughter is clever, good, and beautiful."

"Thank the gentleman for his compliment," said the mother, "for you are really stupid, wanton, and ugly;" and then she added, "But how could you have the face to sit at table with the gentleman in a dirty chemise?"

"I should blush, mother, if I thought you were right; but I put a clean one on only two hours ago."

"Madam," said I to the mother, "the chemise cannot look white beside your daughter's whiter skin."

This made the mother laugh, and pleased the girl immensely. When the mother told her that she was come to take her back, Veronique said, with a sly smile,—

"Perhaps the gentleman won't be pleased at my leaving him twenty-four hours before he goes away."

"On the contrary," said I, "I should be very vexed."

"Well; then, she can stay, sir," said the mother; "but for decency's sake
I must send her younger sister to sleep with her."

"If you please," I rejoined. And with that I left them.

The thought of Veronique troubled me, as I knew I was taken with her, and what I had to dread was a calculated resistance.

The mother came into my room where I was writing, and wished me a pleasant journey, telling me for the second time that she was going to send her daughter Annette. The girl came in the evening, accompanied by a servant, and after lowering her mezzaro, and kissing my hand respectfully, she ran gaily to kiss her sister.

I wanted to see what she was like, and called for candles; and on their being brought I found she was a blonde of a kind I had never before seen. Her hair, eyebrows, and eyelashes were the colour of pale gold, fairer almost than her skin, which was extremely delicate. She was very short-sighted, but her large pale blue eyes were wonderfully beautiful. She had the smallest mouth imaginable, but her teeth, though regular, were not so white as her skin. But for this defect Annette might have passed for a perfect beauty.

Her shortness of sight made too brilliant a light painful to her, but as she stood before me she seemed to like me looking at her. My gaze fed hungrily on the two little half-spheres, which were not yet ripe, but so white as to make me guess how ravishing the rest of her body must be. Veronique did not shew her breasts so freely. One could see that she was superbly shaped, but everything was carefully hidden from the gaze. She made her sister sit down beside her and work, but when I saw that she was obliged to hold the stuff close to her face I told her that she should spare her eyes, for that night at all events, and with that she obediently put the work down.

The marquis came as usual, and like myself he thought Annette, whom he had never seen before, an astonishing miniature beauty. Taking advantage of his age and high rank, the voluptuous old man dared to pass his hand over her breast, and she, who was too respectful to cross my lord, let him do it without making the slightest objection. She was a compound of innocence and coquetry.

The woman who shewing little succeeds in making a man want to see more, has accomplished three-fourths of the task of making him fall in love with her; for is love anything else than a kind of curiosity? I think not; and what makes me certain is that when the curiosity is satisfied the love disappears. Love, however, is the strongest kind of curiosity in existence, and I was already curious about Annette.

M. Grimaldi told Veronique that Rosalie wished her to stay with me till I left Genoa, and she was as much astonished at this as I was.

"Be kind enough to tell her," said I to the marquis, "that Veronique has anticipated her wishes and has got her sister Annette to stay with her."

"Two are always better than one, my dear fellow," replied the crafty Genoese.

After these remarks we left the two sisters together and went into my room, where he said,—

"Your Rosalie is contented, and you ought to congratulate yourself on having made her happy, as I am sure she will be. The only thing that vexes me is that you can't go and see her yourself with any decency."

"You are in love with her, my lord."

"I confess that I am, but I am an old man, and it vexes me."

"That's no matter, she will love you tenderly; and if Petri ever becomes her husband, I am sure she will never be anything more than a good friend to him. Write to me at Florence and tell me how she receives him."

"Stay here for another three days; the two beauties there will make the time seem short."

"It's exactly for that reason that I want to go tomorrow. I am afraid of Veronique."

"I shouldn't have thought that you would have allowed any woman to frighten you."

"I am afraid she has cast her fatal nets around me, and when the time comes she will be strictly moral. Rosalie is my only love."

"Well, here's a letter from her."

I went apart to read the letter, the sight of which made my heart beat violently; it ran as follows:

"Dearest,—I see you have placed me in the hands of one who will care for me like a father. This is a new kindness which I owe to the goodness of your heart. I will write to you at whatever address you send me. If you like Veronique, my darling, do not fear any jealousy from me; I should be wrong to entertain such a feeling in my present position. I expect that if you make much of her she will not be able to resist, and I shall be glad to hear that she is lessening your sadness. I hope you will write me a few lines before you go."

I went up to the marquis and told him to read it. He seemed greatly moved.

"Yes," said he, "the dear girl will find in me her friend and father, and if she marries my godson and he does not treat her as he ought, he will not possess her long. I shall remember her in my will, and thus when I am dead my care will still continue. But what do you think of her advice as to Veronique? I don't expect she is exactly a vestal virgin, though I have never heard anything against her."

I had ordered that the table should be laid for four, so Annette sat down without our having to ask her. Le Duc appeared on the scene, and I told him that if he were ill he might go to bed.

"I am quite well," said he.

"I am glad to hear it; but don't trouble now, you shall wait on me when I am at Leghorn."

I saw that Veronique was delighted at my sending him away, and I resolved then and there to lay siege to her heart. I began by talking to her in a very meaning manner all supper-time, while the marquis entertained Annette. I asked him if he thought I could get a felucca next day to take me to Lerici.

"Yes," said he, "whenever you like and with as many oarsmen as you please; but I hope you will put off your departure for two or three days."

"No," I replied, ogling Veronique, "the delay might cost me too dear."

The sly puss answered with a smile that shewed she understood my meaning.

When we rose from the table I amused myself with Annette, and the marquis with Veronique. After a quarter of an hour he came and said to me,—

"Certain persons have asked me to beg you to stay a few days longer, or at least to sup here to-morrow night."

"Very good. We will talk of the few days more at supper to-morrow."

"Victory!" said the marquis; and Veronique seemed very grateful to me for granting her request. When our guest was gone, I asked my new housekeeper if I might send Costa to bed.

"As my sister is with me, there can be no ground for any suspicion."

"I am delighted that you consent; now I am going to talk to you."

She proceeded to do my hair, but she gave no answer to my soft speeches. When I was on the point of getting into bed she wished me good night, and I tried to kiss her by way of return. She repulsed me and ran to the door, much to my surprise. She was going to leave the room, when I addressed her in a voice of grave politeness.

"I beg you will stay; I want to speak to you; come and sit by me. Why should you refuse me a pleasure which after all is a mere mark of friendship?"

"Because, things being as they are, we could not remain friends, neither could we be lovers."

"Lovers! why not, we are perfectly free."

"I am not free; I am bound by certain prejudices which do not trouble you."

"I should have thought you were superior to prejudices."

"There are some prejudices which a woman ought to respect. The superiority you mention is a pitiful thing; always the dupe of itself. What would become of me, I should like to know, if I abandoned myself to the feelings I have for you?"

"I was waiting for you to say that, dear Veronique. What you feel for me is not love. If it were so, you would feel as I do, and you would soon break the bonds of prejudice."

"I confess that my head is not quite turned yet, but still I feel that I shall grieve at your departure."

"If so, that is no fault of mine. But tell me what I can do for you during my short stay here."

"Nothing; we do not know one another well enough."

"I understand you, but I would have you know that I do not intend to marry any woman who is not my friend."

"You mean you will not marry her till you have ceased to be her lover?"

"Exactly."

"You would like to finish where I would begin."

"You may be happy some day, but you play for high stakes."

"Well, well, it's a case of win all or lose all."

"That's as may be. But without further argument it seems to me that we could safely enjoy our love, and pass many happy moments undisturbed by prejudice."

"Possibly, but one gets burnt fingers at that game, and I shudder at the very thought of it. No, no; leave me alone, there is my sister who will wonder why I am in your arms."

"Very good; I see I was mistaken, and Rosalie too."

"Why what did she think about me?"

"She wrote and told me that she thought you would be kind."

"I hope she' mayn't have to repent for having been too kind herself."

"Good bye, Veronique."

I felt vexed at having made the trial, for in these matters one always feels angry at failure. I decided I would leave her and her precepts, true or false, alone; but when I awoke in the morning and saw her coming to my bed with a pleasant smile on her face, I suddenly changed my mind. I had slept upon my anger and I was in love again. I thought she had repented, and that I should be victorious when I attacked her again. I put on a smile myself and breakfasted gaily with her and her sister. I behaved in the same way at dinner; and the general high spirits which M. de Grimaldi found prevailing in the evening, made him think, doubtless, that we were getting on well, and he congratulated us. Veronique behaved exactly as if the marquis had guessed the truth, and I felt sure of having her after supper, and in the ecstasy of the thought I promised to stay for four days longer.

"Bravo, Veronique!" said the marquis, "that's the way. You are intended by nature to rule your lovers with an absolute sway."

I thought she would say something to diminish the marquis's certainty that there was an agreement between us, but she did nothing of the sort, seeming to enjoy her triumph which made her appear more beautiful than ever; whilst I looked at her with the submissive gaze of a captive who glories in, his chain. I took her behaviour as an omen of my approaching conquest, and did not speak to M. de Grimaldi alone lest he might ask me questions which I should not care to answer. He told us before he went away that he was engaged on the morrow, and so could not come to see us till the day after.

As soon as we were alone Veronique said to me, "You see how I let people believe what they please; I had rather be thought kind, as you call it, than ridiculous, as an honest girl is termed now-a-days. Is it not so?"

"No, dear Veronique, I will never call you ridiculous, but I shall think you hate me if you make me pass another night in torture. You have inflamed me."

"Oh, pray be quiet! For pity's sake leave me alone! I will not inflame you any more. Oh! Oh!"

I had enraged her by thrusting a daring hand into the very door of the sanctuary. She repulsed me and fled. Three or four minutes later her sister came to undress me. I told her gently to go to bed as I had to write for three or four hours; but not caring that she should come on a bootless errand I opened a box and gave her a watch. She took it modestly, saying,—

"This is for my sister, I suppose?"

"No, dear Annette, it's for you."

She gave a skip of delight, and I could not prevent her kissing my hand.

I proceeded to write Rosalie a letter of four pages. I felt worried and displeased with myself and everyone else. I tore up my letter without reading it over, and making an effort to calm myself I wrote her another letter more subdued than the first, in which I said nothing of Veronique, but informed my fair recluse that I was going on the day following.

I did not go to bed till very late, feeling out of temper with the world. I considered that I had failed in my duty to Veronique, whether she loved me or not, for I loved her and I was a man of honour. I had a bad night, and when I awoke it was noon, and on ringing Costa and Annette appeared. The absence of Veronique shewed how I had offended her. When Costa had left the room I asked Annette after her sister, and she said that she was working. I wrote her a note, in which I begged her pardon, promising that I would never offend her again, and begging her to forget everything and to be just the same as before. I was taking my coffee when she came into my room with an expression of mortification which grieved me excessively.

"Forget everything, I beg, and I will trouble you no more. Give me my buckles, as I am going for a country walk, and I shall not be in till suppertime. I shall doubtless get an excellent appetite, and as you have nothing more to fear you need not trouble to send me Annette again."

I dressed myself in haste, and left the town by the first road that came in my way, and I walked fast for two hours with the intention of tiring myself, and of thus readjusting the balance between mind and body. I have always found that severe exercise and fresh air are the best cure for any mental perturbation.

I had walked for more than three leagues when hunger and weariness made me stop at a village inn, where I had an omelette cooked. I ate it hungrily with brown bread and wine, which seemed to me delicious though it was rather sharp.

I felt too tired to walk back to Genoa, so I asked for a carriage; but there was no such thing to be had. The inn-keeper provided me with a sorry nag and a man to guide me. Darkness was coming on, and we had more than six miles to do. Fine rain began to fall when I started, and continued all the way, so that I got home by eight o'clock wet to the skin, shivering with cold, dead tired, and in a sore plight from the rough saddle, against which my satin breeches were no protection. Costa helped me to change my clothes, and as he went out Annette came in.

"Where is your sister?"

"She is in bed with a bad headache. She gave me a letter for you; here it is."

"I have been obliged to go to bed on account of a severe headache to which I am subject. I feel better already, and I shall be able to wait on you to-morrow. I tell you as much, because I do not wish you to think that my illness is feigned. I am sure that your repentance for having humiliated me is sincere, and I hope in your turn that you will forgive me or pity me, if my way of thinking prevents me from conforming to yours."

"Annette dear, go and ask your sister if she would like us to sup in her room."

She soon came back telling me that Veronique was obliged, but begged me to let her sleep.

I supped with Annette, and was glad to see that, though she only drank water, her appetite was better than mine. My passion for her sister prevented me thinking of her, but I felt that Annette would otherwise have taken my fancy. When we were taking dessert, I conceived the idea of making her drunk to get her talk of her sister, so I gave her a glass of Lunel muscat.

"I only drink water, sir."

"Don't you like wine?"

"Yes, but as I am not used to it I am afraid of its getting into my head."

"Then you can go to bed; you will sleep all the better."

She drank the first glass, which she enjoyed immensely, then a second, and then a third. Her little brains were in some confusion when she had finished the third glass. I made her talk about her sister, and in perfect faith she told me all the good imaginable.

"Then you are very fond of Veronique?" said I.

"Oh, yes! I love her with all my heart, but she will not let me caress her."

"No doubt she is afraid of your ceasing to love her. But do you think she ought to make me suffer so?"

"No, but if you love her you ought to forgive her."

Annette was still quite reasonable. I made her drink a fourth glass of muscat, but an instant after she told me that she could not see anything, and we rose from the table. Annette began to please me a little too much, but I determined not to make any attempts upon her for fear of finding her too submissive. A little resistance sharpens the appetite, while favours granted with too much ease lose a great deal of their charm. Annette was only fourteen, she had a soft heart, no knowledge of the world or her own rights, and she would not have resisted my embraces for fear of being rude. That sort of thing would only please a rich and voluptuous Turk.

I begged her to do my hair, intending to dismiss her directly after, but when she had finished I asked her to give me the ointment.

"What do you want it for?"

"For the blisters that cursed saddle on which I rode six miles gave me."

"Does the ointment do them good?"

"Certainly; it takes away the smart, and by to-morrow I shall be cured, but you must send Costa to me, as I cannot put it on myself."

"Can't I do it?"

"Yes, but I am afraid that would be an abuse of your kindness."

"I guess why; but as I am short-sighted, how shall I see the blisters?"

"If you want to do it for me, I will place myself so that it will be easier for you. Stay, put the candle on this table."

"There you are, but don't let Costa put it on again to-morrow, or he will guess that I or my sister did it to-night."

"You will do me the same service, then, to-morrow?"

"I or my sister, for she will get up early."

"Your sister! No, my dear; she would be afraid of giving me too much pleasure by touching me so near."

"And I am only afraid of hurting you. Is that right? Good heavens! what a state your skin is in!"

"You have not finished yet."

"I am so short-sighted; turn round."

"With pleasure. Here I am."

The little wanton could not resist laughing at what she saw, doubtless, for the first time. She was obliged to touch it to continue rubbing the ointment in, and I saw that she liked it, as she touched it when she had no need, and not being able to stand it any longer I took hold of her hand and made her stop her work in favour of a pleasanter employment.   .

When she had finished I burst out laughing to hear her ask, in the most serious way, the pot of ointment still in her left hand,

"Did I do it right!"

"Oh, admirably, dear Annette! You are an angel, and I am sure you know what pleasure you gave me. Can you come and spend an hour with me?"

"Wait a bit."

She went out and shut the door, and I waited for her to return; but my patience being exhausted I opened the door slightly, and saw her undressing and getting into bed with her sister. I went back to my room and to bed again, without losing all hope. I was not disappointed, for in five minutes back she came, clad in her chemise and walking on tip-toe.

"Come to my arms, my love; it is very cold."

"Here I am. My sister is asleep and suspects nothing; and even if she awoke the bed is so large that she would not notice my absence."

"You are a divine creature, and I love you with all my heart."

"So much the better. I give myself up to you; do what you like with me, on the condition that you think of my sister no more."

"That will not cost me much. I promise that I will not think of her."

I found Annette a perfect neophyte, and though I saw no blood on the altar of love next morning I did not suspect her on that account. I have often seen such cases, and I know by experience that the effusion of blood or its absence proves nothing. As a general rule a girl cannot be convicted of having had a lover unless she be with child.

I spent two hours of delight with this pretty baby, for she was so small, so delicate, and so daintily shaped all over, that I can find no better name for her. Her docility did not detract from the piquancy of the pleasure, for she was voluptuously inclined.

When I rose in the morning she came to my room with Veronique, and I was glad to see that while the younger sister was radiant with happiness the elder looked pleasant and as if she desired to make herself agreeable. I asked her how she was, and she told me that diet and sleep had completely cured her. "I have always found them the best remedy for a headache." Annette had also cured me of the curiosity I had felt about her. I congratulated myself on my achievement.

I was in such high spirits at supper that M. de Grimaldi thought I had won everything from Veronique, and I let him think so. I promised to dine with him the next day, and I kept my word. After dinner I gave him a long letter for Rosalie, whom I did not expect to see again except as Madame Petri, though I took care not to let the marquis know what I thought.

In the evening I supped with the two sisters, and I made myself equally agreeable to both of them. When Veronique was alone with me, putting my hair into curl-papers, she said that she loved me much more now that I behaved discreetly.

"My discretion," I replied, "only means that I have given up the hope of winning you. I know how to take my part."

"Your love was not very great, then?"

"It sprang up quickly, and you, Veronique, could have made it increase to a gigantic size."

She said nothing, but bit her lip, wished me good night and left the room. I went to bed expecting a visit from Annette, but I waited in vain. When I rang the next morning the dear girl appeared looking rather sad. I asked her the reason.

"Because my sister is ill, and spent the whole night in writing," said she.

Thus I learnt the reason of her not having paid me a visit.

"Do you know what she was writing about?"

"Oh, no! She does not tell me that kind of thing, but here is a letter for you."

I read through the long and well-composed letter, but as it bore marks of craft and dissimulation it made me laugh. After several remarks of no consequence she said that she had repulsed me because she loved me so much and that she was afraid that if she satisfied my fancy she might lose me.

"I will be wholly yours," she added, "if you will give me the position which Rosalie enjoyed. I will travel in your company, but you must give me a document, which M. de Grimaldi will sign as a witness, in which you must engage to marry me in a year, and to give me a portion of fifty thousand francs; and if at the end of a year you do not wish to marry me, that sum to be at my absolute disposal."

She stipulated also that if she became a mother in the course of a year the child should be hers in the event of our separating. On these conditions she would become my mistress, and would have for me all possible love and kindness.

This proposal, cleverly conceived, but foolishly communicated to me, shewed me that Veronique had not the talent of duping others. I saw directly that M. de Grimaldi had nothing to do with it, and I felt sure that he would laugh when I told him the story.

Annette soon came back with the chocolate, and told me that her sister hoped I would answer her letter.

"Yes, dear," said I, "I will answer her when I get up."

I took my chocolate, put on my dressing-gown, and went to Veronique's room. I found her sitting up in bed in a negligent attire that might have attracted me if her letter had not deprived her of my good opinion. I sat on the bed, gave her back the letter, and said,—

"Why write, when we can talk the matter over?"

"Because one is often more at ease in writing than in speaking."

"In diplomacy and business that will pass, but not in love. Love makes no conditions. Let us have no documents, no safeguards, but give yourself up to me as Rosalie did, and begin to-night without my promising anything. If you trust in love, you will make him your prisoner. That way will honour us and our pleasures, and if you like I will consult M. de Grimaldi on the subject. As to your plan, if it does not injure your honour, it does small justice to your common sense, and no one but a fool would agree to it. You could not possibly love the man to whom you make such a proposal, and as to M. de Grimaldi, far from having anything to do with it, I am sure he would be indignant at the very idea."

This discourse did not put Veronique out of countenance. She said she did not love me well enough to give herself to me unconditionally; to which I replied that I was not sufficiently taken with her charms to buy them at the price she fixed, and so I left her.

I called Costa, and told him to go and warn the master of the felucca that I was going the next day, and with this idea I went to bid good-bye to the marquis, who informed me that he had just been taking Petri to see Rosalie, who had received him well enough. I told him I was glad to hear it, and said that I commended to him the care of her happiness, but such commendations were thrown away.

It is one of the most curious circumstances of my history, that in one year two women whom I sincerely loved and whom I might have married were taken from me by two old men, whose affections I had fostered without wishing to do so. Happily these gentlemen made my mistresses' fortunes, but on the other hand they did me a still greater service in relieving me of a tie which I should have found very troublesome in course of time. No doubt they both saw that my fortune, though great in outward show, rested on no solid basis, which, as the reader will see, was unhappily too true. I should be happy if I thought that my errors or rather follies would serve as a warning to the readers of these Memoirs.

I spent the day in watching the care with which Veronique and Annette packed up my trunks, for I would not let my two servants help in any way. Veronique was neither sad nor gay. She looked as if she had made up her mind, and as if there had never been any differences between us. I was very glad, for as I no longer cared for her I should have been annoyed to find that she still cared for me.

We supped in our usual manner, discussing only commonplace topics, but just as I was going to bed Annette shook my hand in a way that told me to prepare for a visit from her. I admired the natural acuteness of young girls, who take their degrees in the art of love with so much ease and at such an early age. Annette, almost a child, knew more than a young man of twenty. I decided on giving her fifty sequins without letting Veronique see me, as I did not intend to be so liberal towards her. I took a roll of ducats and gave them to her as soon as she came.

She lay down beside me, and after a moment devoted to love she said that Veronique was asleep, adding,—

"I heard all you said to my sister, and I am sure you love her."

"If I did, dear Annette, I should not have made my proposal in such plain terms."

"I should like to believe that, but what would you have done if she had accepted your offer? You would be in one bed by this, I suppose?"

"I was more than certain, dearest, that her pride would hinder her receiving me."

We had reached this point in our conversation when we were surprised by the sudden appearance of Veronique with a lighted candle, and wearing only her chemise. She laughed at her sister to encourage her, and I joined in the laughter, keeping a firm hold on the little one for fear of her escaping. Veronique looked ravishing in her scanty attire, and as she laughed I could not be angry with her. However, I said,—

"You have interrupted our enjoyment, and hurt your sister's feelings; perhaps you will despise her for the future?"

"On the contrary, I shall always love her."

"Her feelings overcame her, and she surrendered to me without making any terms."

"She has more sense than I."

"Do you mean that?"

"I do, really."

"I am astonished and delighted to hear it; but as it is so, kiss your sister."

At this invitation Veronique put down the candle, and covered Annette's beautiful body with kisses. The scene made me feel very happy.

"Come, Veronique," said I, "you will die of cold; come and lie down."

I made room for her, and soon there were three of us under the same sheet. I was in an ecstasy at this group, worthy of Aretin's pencil.

"Dearest ones," said I, "you have played me a pretty trick; was it premeditated? And was Veronique false this morning, or is she false now?"

"We did not premeditate anything, I was true this morning, and I am true now. I feel that I and my plan were very silly, and I hope you will forgive me, since I have repented and have had my punishment. Now I think I am in my right senses, as I have yielded to the feelings with which you inspired me when I saw you first, and against which I have fought too long."

"What you say pleases me extremely."

"Well, forgive me and finish my punishment by shewing that you are not angry with me."

"How am I to do that?"

"By telling me that you are vexed no longer, and by continuing to give my sister proofs of your love."

"I swear to you that so far from being angry with you I am very fond of you; but would you like us to be fond in your presence?"

"Yes, if you don't mind me."

Feeling excited by voluptuous emotions, I saw that my part could no longer be a passive one.

"What do you say," said I to my blonde, "will you allow your heroic sister to remain a mere looker-on at our sweet struggles? Are you not generous enough to let me make her an actress in the drama?"

"No; I confess I do not feel as if I could be so generous to-night, but next night, if you will play the same part, we will change. Veronique shall act and I will look on."

"That would do beautifully," said Veronique, with some vexation in her manner, "if the gentleman was not going to-morrow morning."

"I will stay, dear Veronique, if only to prove how much I love you."

I could not have wished for plainer speech on her part, and I should have liked to shew her how grateful I felt on the spot; but that would have been at Annette's expense, as I had no right to make any alteration in the piece of which she was the author and had a right to expect all the profits. Whenever I recall this pleasant scene I feel my heart beat with voluptuous pleasure, and even now, with the hand of old age upon me, I can not recall it without delight.

Veronique resigned herself to the passive part which her younger sister imposed on her, and turning aside she leant her head on her hand, disclosing a breast which would have excited the coldest of men, and bade me begin my attack on Annette. It was no hard task she laid upon me, for I was all on fire, and I was certain of pleasing her as long as she looked at me. As Annette was short-sighted, she could not distinguish in the heat of the action which way I was looking, and I succeeded in getting my right hand free, without her noticing me, and I was thus enabled to communicate a pleasure as real though not as acute as that enjoyed by her sister. When the coverlet was disarranged, Veronique took the trouble to replace it, and thus offered me, as if by accident, a new spectacle. She saw how I enjoyed the sight of her charms, and her eye brightened. At last, full of unsatisfied desire, she shewed me all the treasures which nature had given her, just as I had finished with Annette for the fourth time. She might well think that I was only rehearsing for the following night, and her fancy must have painted her coming joys in the brightest colours. Such at all events were my thoughts, but the fates determined otherwise. I was in the middle of the seventh act, always slower and more pleasant for the actress than the first two or three, when Costa came knocking loudly at my door, calling out that the felucca was ready. I was vexed at this untoward incident, got up in a rage, and after telling him to pay the master for the day, as I was not going till the morrow, I went back to bed, no longer, however, in a state to continue the work I begun. My two sweethearts were delighted with me, but we all wanted rest, though the piece should not have finished with an interruption. I wanted to get some amusement out of the interval, and proposed an ablution, which made Annette laugh and which Veronique pronounced to be absolutely necessary. I found it a delicious hors d'oeuvre to the banquet I had enjoyed. The two sisters rendered each other various services, standing in the most lascivious postures, and I found my situation as looker-on an enviable one.

When the washing and the laughter it gave rise to were over, we returned to the stage where the last act should have been performed. I longed to begin again, and I am sure I should have succeeded if I had been well backed up by my partner; but Annette, who was young and tired out with the toils of the night, forgot her part, and yielded to sleep as she had yielded to love. Veronique began to laugh when she saw her asleep, and I had to do the same, when I saw that she was as still as a corpse.

"What a pity!" said Veronique's eyes; but she said it with her eyes alone, while I was waiting for these words to issue from her lips. We were both of us wrong: she for not speaking, and I for waiting for her to speak. It was a favourable moment, but we let it pass by, and love punished us. I had, it is true, another reason for abstaining. I wished to reserve myself for the night. Veronique went to her own bed to quiet her excited feelings, and I stayed in bed with my sleeping beauty till noon, when I wished her good morning by a fresh assault which was completed neither on her side nor on mine to the best of my belief.

The day was spent in talking about ourselves, and determined to eat only one meal, we did not sit down to table till night began to fall. We spent two hours in the consumption of delicate dishes, and in defying Bacchus to make us feel his power. We rose as we saw Annette falling asleep, but we were not much annoyed at the thought that she would not see the pleasures we promised each other. I thought that I should have enough to do to contemplate the charms of the one nymph without looking at Annette's beauties. We went to bed, our arms interlaced, our bodies tight together, and lip pressed on lip, but that was all. Veronique saw what prevented me going any further, and she was too polite and modest to complain. She dissembled her feelings and continued to caress me, while I was in a frenzy of rage. I had never had such a misfortune, unless as the result of complete exhaustion, or from a strong mental impression capable of destroying my natural faculties. Let my readers imagine what I suffered; in the flower of my age, with a strong constitution, holding the body of a woman I had ardently desired in my arms, while she tenderly caressed me, and yet I could do nothing for her. I was in despair; one cannot offer a greater insult to a woman.

At last we had to accept the facts and speak reasonably, and I was the first to bewail my misfortune.

"You tired yourself too much yesterday," said she, "and you were not sufficiently temperate at supper. Do not let it trouble you, dearest, I am sure you love me. Do not try to force nature, you will only weaken yourself more. I think a gentle sleep would restore your manly powers better than anything. I can't sleep myself, but don't mind me. Sleep, we will make love together afterwards."

After those excellent and reasonable suggestions, Veronique turned her back to me and I followed her example, but in vain did I endeavour to obtain a refreshing slumber; nature which would not give me the power of making her, the loveliest creature, happy, envied me the power of repose as well. My amorous ardour and my rage forbade all thoughts of rest, and my excited passions conspired against that which would enable them to satisfy their desires. Nature punished me for having distrusted her, and because I had taken stimulants fit only for the weak. If I had fasted, I should have done great things, but now there was a conflict between the stimulants and nature, and by my desire for enjoyment I had deprived myself of the power to enjoy. Thus nature, wise like its Divine Author, punishes the ignorance and presumption of poor weak mortals.

Throughout this terrible and sleepless night my mind roamed abroad, and amidst the reproaches with which I overwhelmed myself I found a certain satisfaction in the thought that they were not wholly undeserved. This is the sole enjoyment I still have when I meditate on my past life and its varied adventures. I feel that no misfortune has befallen me save by my own fault, whilst I attribute to natural causes the blessings, of which I have enjoyed many. I think I should go mad if in my soliloquies I came across any misfortune which I could not trace to my own fault, for I should not know where to place the reason, and that would degrade me to the rank of creatures governed by instinct alone. I feel that I am somewhat more than a beast. A beast, in truth, is a foolish neighbour of mine, who tries to argue that the brutes reason better than we do.

"I will grant," I said, "that they reason better than you, but I can go no farther; and I think every reasonable man would say as much."

This reply has made me an enemy, although he admits the first part of the thesis.

Happier than I, Veronique slept for three hours; but she was disagreeably surprised on my telling her that I had not been able to close an eye, and on finding me in the same state of impotence as before. She began to get angry when I tried to convince her rather too forcibly that my misfortune was not due to my want of will, and then she blamed herself as the cause of my impotence; and mortified by the idea, she endeavoured to destroy the spell by all the means which passion suggested, and which I had hitherto thought infallible; but her efforts and mine were all thrown away. My despair was as great as hers when at last, wearied, ashamed, and degraded in her own eyes, she discontinued her efforts, her eyes full of tears. She went away without a word, and left me alone for the two or three hours which had still to elapse before the dawn appeared.

At day-break Costa came and told me that the sea being rough and a contrary wind blowing, the felucca would be in danger of perishing.

"We will go as soon as the weather improves," said I; "in the mean time light me a fire."

I arose, and proceeded to write down the sad history of the night. This occupation soothed me, and feeling inclined to sleep I lay down again and slept for eight hours. When I awoke I felt better, but still rather sad. The two sisters were delighted to see me in good health, but I thought I saw on Veronique's features an unpleasant expression of contempt. However, I had deserved it, and I did not take the trouble of changing her opinion, though if she had been more caressing she might easily have put me in a state to repair the involuntary wrongs I had done her in the night. Before we sat down to table I gave her a present of a hundred sequins, which made her look a little more cheerful. I gave an equal present to my dear Annette, who had not expected anything, thinking herself amply recompensed by my first gift and by the pleasure I had afforded her.

At midnight the master of the felucca came to tell me that the wind had changed, and I took leave of the sisters. Veronique shed tears, but I knew to what to attribute them. Annette kissed me affectionately; thus each played her own part. I sailed for Lerici, where I arrived the next day, and then posted to Leghorn. Before I speak of this town I think I shall interest my readers by narrating a circumstance not unworthy of these Memoirs.

CHAPTER VI

A Clever Cheat—Passano—Pisa—Corilla—My Opinion of Squinting Eyes—Florence—I See Therese Again—My Son—Corticelli

I was standing at some distance from my carriage into which they were putting four horses, when a man accosted me and asked me if I would pay in advance or at the next stage. Without troubling to look at him I said I would pay in advance, and gave him a coin requesting him to bring me the change.

"Directly, sir," said he, and with that he went into the inn.

A few minutes after, just as I was going to look after my change, the post-master came up and asked me to pay for the stage.

"I have paid already, and I am waiting for my change. Did I not give the money to you?"

"Certainly not, sir."

"Whom did I give it to, then?"

"I really can't say; but you will be able to recognize the man, doubtless."

"It must have been you or one of your people."

I was speaking loud, and all the men came about me.

"These are all the men in my employ," said the master, and he asked if any of them had received the money from me.

They all denied the fact with an air of sincerity which left no room for suspicion. I cursed and swore, but they let me curse and swear as much as I liked. At last I discovered that there was no help for it, and I paid a second time, laughing at the clever rascal who had taken me in so thoroughly. Such are the lessons of life; always full of new experiences, and yet one never knows enough. From that day I have always taken care not to pay for posting except to the proper persons.

In no country are knaves so cunning as in Italy, Greece ancient and modern excepted.

When I got to the best inn at Leghorn they told me that there was a theatre, and my luck made me go and see the play. I was recognized by an actor who accosted me, and introduced me to one of his comrades, a self-styled poet, and a great enemy of the Abbe Chiari, whom I did not like, as he had written a biting satire against me, and I had never succeeded in avenging myself on him. I asked them to come and sup with me—a windfall which these people are not given to refusing. The pretended poet was a Genoese, and called himself Giacomo Passano. He informed me that he had written three hundred sonnets against the abbe, who would burst with rage if they were ever printed. As I could not restrain a smile at the good opinion the poet had of his works, he offered to read me a few sonnets. He had the manuscript about him, and I could not escape the penance. He read a dozen or so, which I thought mediocre, and a mediocre sonnet is necessarily a bad sonnet, as this form of poetry demands sublimity; and thus amongst the myriads of sonnets to which Italy gives birth very few can be called good.

If I had given myself time to examine the man's features, I should, no doubt, have found him to be a rogue; but I was blinded by passion, and the idea of three hundred sonnets against the Abbe Chiari fascinated me.

I cast my eyes over the title of the manuscript, and read, "La Chiareide di Ascanio Pogomas."

"That's an anagram of my Christian name and my surname; is it not a happy combination?"

This folly made me smile again. Each of the sonnets was a dull diatribe ending with "l'abbate Chiari e un coglione." He did not prove that he was one, but he said so over and over again, making use of the poet's privilege to exaggerate and lie. What he wanted to do was to annoy the abbe, who was by no means what Passano called him, but on the contrary, a wit and a poet; and if he had been acquainted with the requirements of the stage he would have written better plays than Goldoni, as he had a greater command of language.

I told Passano, for civility's sake, that he ought to get his Chiareide printed.

"I would do so," said he, "if I could find a publisher, for I am not rich enough to pay the expenses, and the publishers are a pack of ignorant beggars. Besides, the press is not free, and the censor would not let the epithet I give to my hero pass. If I could go to Switzerland I am sure it could be managed; but I must have six sequins to walk to Switzerland, and I have not got them."

"And when you got to Switzerland, where there are no theatres, what would you do for a living?"

"I would paint in miniature. Look at those."

He gave me a number of small ivory tablets, representing obscene subjects, badly drawn and badly painted.

"I will give you an introduction to a gentleman at Berne," I said; and after supper I gave him a letter and six sequins. He wanted to force some of his productions on me, but I would not have them.

I was foolish enough to give him a letter to pretty Sara's father, and I told him to write to me at Rome, under cover of the banker Belloni.

I set out from Leghorn the next day and went to Pisa, where I stopped two days. There I made the acquaintance of an Englishman, of whom I bought a travelling carriage. He took me to see Corilla, the celebrated poetess. She received me with great politeness, and was kind enough to improvise on several subjects which I suggested. I was enchanted, not so much with her grace and beauty, as by her wit and perfect elocution. How sweet a language sounds when it is spoken well and the expressions are well chosen. A language badly spoken is intolerable even from a pretty mouth, and I have always admired the wisdom of the Greeks who made their nurses teach the children from the cradle to speak correctly and pleasantly. We are far from following their good example; witness the fearful accents one hears in what is called, often incorrectly, good society.

Corilla was 'straba', like Venus as painted by the ancients—why, I cannot think, for however fair a squint-eyed woman may be otherwise, I always look upon her face as distorted. I am sure that if Venus had been in truth a goddess, she would have made the eccentric Greek, who first dared to paint her cross-eyed, feel the weight of her anger. I was told that when Corilla sang, she had only to fix her squinting eyes on a man and the conquest was complete; but, praised be God! she did not fix them on me.

At Florence I lodged at the "Hotel Carrajo," kept by Dr. Vannini, who delighted to confess himself an unworthy member of the Academy Della Crusca. I took a suite of rooms which looked out on the bank of the Arno. I also took a carriage and a footman, whom, as well as a coachman, I clad in blue and red livery. This was M. de Bragadin's livery, and I thought I might use his colours, not with the intention of deceiving anyone, but merely to cut a dash.

The morning after my arrival I put on my great coat to escape observation, and proceeded to walk about Florence. In the evening I went to the theatre to see the famous harlequin, Rossi, but I considered his reputation was greater than he deserved. I passed the same judgment on the boasted Florentine elocution; I did not care for it at all. I enjoyed seeing Pertici; having become old, and not being able to sing any more, he acted, and, strange to say, acted well; for, as a rule, all singers, men and women, trust to their voice and care nothing for acting, so that an ordinary cold entirely disables them for the time being.

Next day I called on the banker, Sasso Sassi, on whom I had a good letter of credit, and after an excellent dinner I dressed and went to the opera an via della Pergola, taking a stage box, not so much for the music, of which I was never much of an admirer, as because I wanted to look at the actress.

The reader may guess my delight and surprise when I recognised in the prima donna Therese, the false Bellino, whom I had left at Rimini in the year 1744; that charming Therese whom I should certainly have married if M. de Gages had not put me under arrest. I had not seen her for seventeen years, but she looked as beautiful and ravishing as ever as she came forward on the stage. It seemed impossible. I could not believe my eyes, thinking the resemblance must be a coincidence, when, after singing an air, she fixed her eyes on mine and kept them there. I could no longer doubt that it was she; she plainly recognized me. As she left the stage she stopped at the wings and made a sign to me with her fan to come and speak to her.

I went out with a beating heart, though I could not explain my perturbation, for I did not feel guilty in any way towards Therese, save in that I had not answered the last letter she had written me from Naples, thirteen years ago. I went round the theatre, feeling a greater curiosity as to the results of our interview than to know what had befallen her during the seventeen years which seemed an age to me.

I came to the stage-door, and I saw Therese standing at the top of the stair. She told the door-keeper to let me pass; I went up and we stood face to face. Dumb with surprise I took her hand and pressed it against my heart.

"Know from that beating heart," said I, "all that I feel."

"I can't follow your example," said she, "but when I saw you I thought I should have fainted. Unfortunately I am engaged to supper. I shall not shut my eyes all night. I shall expect you at eight o'clock to-morrow morning. Where are you staying?"

"At Dr. Vannini's."

"Under what name?"

"My own."

"How long have you been here?"

"Since yesterday."

"Are you stopping long in Florence?"

"As long as you like."

"Are you married?"

"No."

"Cursed be that supper! What an event! You must leave me now, I have to go on. Good-bye till seven o'clock to-morrow."

She had said eight at first, but an hour sooner was no harm. I returned to the theatre, and recollected that I had neither asked her name or address, but I could find out all that easily. She was playing Mandane, and her singing and acting were admirable. I asked a well-dressed young man beside me what that admirable actress's name was.

"You have only come to Florence to-day, sir?"

"I arrived yesterday."

"Ah! well, then it's excusable. That actress has the same name as I have.
She is my wife, and I am Cirillo Palesi, at your service."

I bowed and was silent with surprise. I dared not ask where she lived, lest he might think my curiosity impertinent. Therese married to this handsome young man, of whom, of all others, I had made enquiries about her! It was like a scene in a play.

I could bear it no longer. I longed to be alone and to ponder over this strange adventure at my ease, and to think about my visit to Therese at seven o'clock the next morning. I felt the most intense curiosity to see what the husband would do when he recognized me, and he was certain to do so, for he had looked at me attentively as he spoke. I felt that my old flame for Therese was rekindled in my heart, and I did not know whether I was glad or sorry at her being married.

I left the opera-house and told my footman to call my carriage.

"You can't have it till nine o'clock, sir; it was so cold the coachman sent the horses back to the stable."

"We will return on foot, then."

"You will catch a cold."

"What is the prima donna's name?"

"When she came here, she called herself Lanti, but for the last two months she has been Madame Palesi. She married a handsome young man with no property and no profession, but she is rich, so he takes his ease and does nothing."

"Where does she live?"

"At the end of this street. There's her house, sir; she lodges on the first floor."

This was all I wanted to know, so I said no more, but took note of the various turnings, that I might be able to find my way alone the next day. I ate a light supper, and told Le Duc to call me at six o'clock.

"But it is not light till seven."

"I know that."

"Very good."

At the dawn of day, I was at the door of the woman I had loved so passionately. I went to the first floor, rang the bell, and an old woman came out and asked me if I were M. Casanova. I told her that I was, whereupon she said that the lady had informed her I was not coming till eight.

"She said seven."

"Well, well, it's of no consequence. Kindly walk in here. I will go and awake her."

In five minutes, the young husband in his night-cap and dressing-gown came in, and said that his wife would not be long. Then looking at me attentively with an astounded stare, he said,

"Are you not the gentleman who asked me my wife's name last night?"

"You are right, I did. I have not seen your wife for many years, but I thought I recognized her. My good fortune made me enquire of her husband, and the friendship which formerly attached me to her will henceforth attach me to you."

As I uttered this pretty compliment Therese, as fair as love, rushed into the room with open arms. I took her to my bosom in a transport of delight, and thus we remained for two minutes, two friends, two lovers, happy to see one another after a long and sad parting. We kissed each other again and again, and then bidding her husband sit down she drew me to a couch and gave full course to her tears. I wept too, and my tears were happy ones. At last we wiped our eyes, and glanced towards the husband whom we had completely forgotten. He stood in an attitude of complete astonishment, and we burst out laughing. There was something so comic in his surprise that it would have taxed all the talents of the poet and the caricaturist to depict his expression of amazement. Therese, who knew how to manage him, cried in a pathetic an affectionate voice,—

"My dear Palesi, you see before you my father—nay, more than a father, for this is my generous friend to whom I owe all. Oh, happy moment for which my heart has longed for these ten years past."

At the word "father" the unhappy husband fixed his gaze on me, but I restrained my laughter with considerable difficulty. Although Therese was young for her age, she was only two years younger than I; but friendship gives a new meaning to the sweet name of father.

"Yes, sir," said I, "your Therese is my daughter, my sister, my cherished friend; she is an angel, and this treasure is your wife."

"I did not reply to your last letter," said I, not giving him time to come to himself.

"I know all," she replied. "You fell in love with a nun. You were imprisoned under the Leads, and I heard of your almost miraculous flight at Vienna. I had a false presentiment that I should see you in that town. Afterwards I heard of you in Paris and Holland, but after you left Paris nobody could tell me any more about you. You will hear some fine tales when I tell you all that has happened to me during the past ten years. Now I am happy. I have my dear Palesi here, who comes from Rome. I married him a couple of months ago. We are very fond of each other, and I hope you will be as much his friend as mine."

At this I arose and embraced the husband, who cut such an extraordinary figure. He met me with open arms, but in some confusion; he was, no doubt, not yet quite satisfied as to the individual who was his wife's father, brother, friend, and perhaps lover, all at once. Therese saw this feeling in his eyes, and after I had done she came and kissed him most affectionately, which confused me in my turn, for I felt all my old love for her renewed, and as ardent as it was when Don Sancio Pico introduced me to her at Ancona.

Reassured by my embrace and his wife's caress, M. Palesi asked me if I would take a cup of chocolate with them, which he himself would make. I answered that chocolate was my favourite breakfast-dish, and all the more so when it was made by a friend. He went away to see to it. Our time had come.

As soon as we were alone Therese threw herself into my arms, her face shining with such love as no pen can describe.

"Oh, my love! whom I shall love all my life, clasp me to your breast! Let us give each other a hundred embraces on this happy day, but not again, since my fate has made me another's bride. To-morrow we will be like brother and sister; to-day let us be lovers."

She had not finished this speech before my bliss was crowned. Our transports were mutual, and we renewed them again and again during the half hour in which we had no fear of an interruption. Her negligent morning dress and my great coat were highly convenient under the circumstances.

After we had satiated in part our amorous ardour we breathed again and sat down. There was a short pause, and then she said,

"You must know that I am in love with my husband and determined not to deceive him. What I have just done was a debt I had to pay to the remembrance of my first love. I had to pay it to prove how much I love you; but let us forget it now. You must be contented with the thought of my great affection for you—of which you can have no doubt—and let me still think that you love me; but henceforth do not let us be alone together, as I should give way, and that would vex me. What makes you look so sad?"

"I find you bound, while I am free. I thought we had met never to part again; you had kindled the old fires. I am the same to you as I was at Ancona. I have proved as much, and you can guess how sad I feel at your decree that I am to enjoy you no more. I find that you are not only married but in love with your husband. Alas! I have come too late, but if I had not stayed at Genoa I should not have been more fortunate. You shall know all in due time, and in the meanwhile I will be guided by you in everything. I suppose your husband knows nothing of our connection, and my best plan will be to be reserved, will it not?"

"Yes, dearest, for he knows nothing of my affairs, and I am glad to say he shews no curiosity respecting them. Like everybody else, he knows I made my fortune at Naples; I told him I went there when I was ten years old. That was an innocent lie which hurts nobody; and in my position I find that inconvenient truths have to give way to lies. I give myself out as only twenty-four, how do you think I look?"

"You look as if you were telling the truth, though I know you must be thirty-two."

"You mean thirty-one, for when I knew you I couldn't have been more than fourteen."

"I thought you were fifteen at least."

"Well, I might admit that between ourselves; but tell me if I look more than twenty-four."

"I swear to you you don't look as old, but at Naples . . . ."

"At Naples some people might be able to contradict me, but nobody would mind them. But I am waiting for what ought to be the sweetest moment of your life."

"What is that, pray?"

"Allow me to keep my own counsel, I want to enjoy your surprise. How are you off? If you want money, I can give you back all you gave me, and with compound interest. All I have belongs to me; my husband is not master of anything. I have fifty thousand ducats at Naples, and an equal sum in diamonds. Tell me how much you want—quick! the chocolate is coming."

Such a woman was Therese. I was deeply moved, and was about to throw my arms about her neck without answering when the chocolate came. Her husband was followed by a girl of exquisite beauty, who carried three cups of chocolate on a silver-gilt dish. While we drank it Palesi amused us by telling us with much humour how surprised he was when he recognized the man who made him rise at such an early hour as the same who had asked him his wife's name the night before. Therese and I laughed till our sides ached, the story was told so wittily and pleasantly. This

Roman displeased me less than I expected; his jealousy seemed only put on for form's sake.

"At ten o'clock," said Theresa, "I have a rehearsal here of the new opera. You can stay and listen if you like. I hope you will dine with us every day, and it will give me great pleasure if you will look upon my house as yours."

"To-day," said I, "I will stay with you till after supper, and then I will leave you with your fortunate husband."

As I pronounced these words M. Palesi embraced me with effusion, as if to thank me for not objecting to his enjoying his rights as a husband.

He was between the ages of twenty and twenty-two, of a fair complexion, and well-made, but too pretty for a man. I did not wonder at Therese being in love with him, for I knew too well the power of a handsome face; but I thought that she had made a mistake in marrying him, for a husband acquires certain rights which may become troublesome.

Therese's pretty maid came to tell me that my carriage was at the door.

"Will you allow me," said I to her, "to have my footman in?"

"Rascal," said I, as soon as he came in, "who told you to come here with my carriage?"

"Nobody, sir, but I know my duty."

"Who told you that I was here?"

"I guessed as much."

"Go and fetch Le Duc, and come back with him."

When they arrived I told Le Duc to pay the impertinent fellow three days' wages, to strip him of his livery, and to ask Dr. Vannini to get me a servant of the same build, not gifted with the faculty of divination, but who knew how to obey his master's orders. The rascal was much perturbed at the result of his officiousness, and asked Therese to plead for him; but, like a sensible woman, she told him that his master was the best judge of the value of his services.

At ten o'clock all the actors and actresses arrived, bringing with them a mob of amateurs who crowded the hall. Therese received their greetings graciously, and I could see she enjoyed a great reputation. The rehearsal lasted three hours, and wearied me extremely. To relieve my boredom I talked to Palesi, whom I liked for not asking me any particulars of my acquaintance with his wife. I saw that he knew how to behave in the position in which he was placed.

A girl from Parma, named Redegonde, who played a man's part and sang very well, stayed to dinner. Therese had also asked a young Bolognese, named Corticelli. I was struck with the budding charms of this pretty dancer, but as I was just then full of Therese, I did not pay much attention to her. Soon after we sat down I saw a plump abbe coming in with measured steps. He looked to me a regular Tartuffe, after nothing but Therese. He came up to her as soon as he saw her, and going on one knee in the Portuguese fashion, kissed her hand tenderly and respectfully. Therese received him with smiling courtesy and put him at her right hand; I was at their left. His voice, manner, and all about him told me that I had known him, and in fact I soon recognized him as the Abbe Gama, whom I had left at Rome seventeen years before with Cardinal Acquaviva; but I pretended not to recognize him, and indeed he had aged greatly. This gallant priest had eyes for no one but Therese, and he was too busy with saying a thousand soft nothings to her to take notice of anybody else in the company. I hoped that in his turn he would either not recognize me or pretend not to do so, so I was continuing my trifling talk with the Corticelli, when Therese told me that the abbe wanted to know whether I did not recollect him. I looked at his face attentively, and with the air of a man who is trying to recollect something, and then I rose and asked if he were not the Abbe Gama, with whose acquaintance I was honoured.

"The same," said he, rising, and placing his arms round my neck he kissed me again and again. This was in perfect agreement with his crafty character; the reader will not have forgotten the portrait of him contained in the first volume of these Memoirs.

After the ice had been thus broken it will be imagined that we had a long conversation. He spoke of Barbaruccia, of the fair Marchioness G——, of Cardinal S—— C——, and told me how he had passed from the Spanish to the Portuguese service, in which he still continued. I was enjoying his talk about numerous subjects which had interested me in my early youth, when an unexpected sight absorbed all my thinking faculties. A young man of fifteen or sixteen, as well grown as Italians usually are at that age, came into the room, saluted the company with easy grace, and kissed Therese. I was the only person who did not know him, but I was not the only one who looked surprised. The daring Therese introduced him to me with perfect coolness with the words:—

"That is my brother."

I greeted him as warmly as I could, but my manner was slightly confused, as I had not had time to recover my composure. This so-called brother of Therese was my living image, though his complexion was rather clearer than mine. I saw at once that he was my son; nature had never been so indiscreet as in the amazing likeness between us. This, then, was the surprise of which Therese had spoken; she had devised the pleasure of seeing me at once astounded and delighted, for she knew that my heart would be touched at the thought of having left her such a pledge of our mutual love. I had not the slightest foreknowledge in the matter, for Therese had never alluded to her being with child in her letters. I thought, however, that she should not have brought about this meeting in the presence of a third party, for everyone has eyes in their head, and anyone with eyes must have seen that the young man was either my son or my brother. I glanced at her, but she avoided meeting my eye, while the pretended brother was looking at me so attentively that he did not hear what was said to him. As to the others, they did nothing but look first at me and then at him, and if they came to the conclusion that he was my son they would be obliged to suppose that I had been the lover of Therese's mother, if she were really his sister, for taking into consideration the age she looked and gave herself out to be she could not possibly be his mother. It was equally impossible that I could be Therese's father, as I did not look any older than she did.

My son spoke the Neapolitan dialect perfectly, but he also spoke Italian very well, and in whatever he said I was glad to recognize taste, good sense, and intelligence. He was well-informed, though he had been brought up at Naples, and his manners were very distinguished. His mother made him sit between us at table.

"His favourite amusement," she said to me, "is music. You must hear him on the clavier, and though I am eight years older I shall not be surprised if you pronounce him the better performer."

Only a woman's delicate instinct could have suggested this remark; men hardly ever approach women in this respect.

Whether from natural impulses or self-esteem, I rose from the table so delighted with my son that I embraced him with the utmost tenderness, and was applauded by the company. I asked everybody to dine with me the next day, and my invitation was joyfully accepted; but the Corticelli said, with the utmost simplicity,

"May I come, too?"

"Certainty; you too."

After dinner the Abbe Gama asked me to breakfast with him, or to have him to breakfast the next morning, as he was longing for a good talk with me.

"Come and breakfast with me," said I, "I shall be delighted to see you."

When the guests had gone Don Cesarino, as the pretended brother of Therese was called, asked me if I would walk with him. I kissed him, and replied that my carriage was at his service, and that he and his brother-in-law could drive in it, but that I had resolved not to leave his sister that day. Palesi seemed quite satisfied with the arrangement, and they both went away.

When we were alone, I gave Therese an ardent embrace, and congratulated her on having such a brother.

"My dear, he is the fruit of our amours; he is your son. He makes me happy, and is happy himself, and indeed he has everything to make him so."

"And I, too, am happy, dear Therese. You must have seen that I recognized him at once."

"But do you want to give him a brother? How ardent you are!"

"Remember, beloved one, that to-morrow we are to be friends, and nothing more."

By this my efforts were crowned with success, but the thought that it was the last time was a bitter drop in the cup of happiness.

When we had regained our composure, Therese said,—

"The duke who took me from Rimini brought up our child; as soon as I knew that I was pregnant I confided my secret to him. No one knew of my delivery, and the child was sent to nurse at Sorrento, and the duke had him baptized under the name of Caesar Philip Land. He remained at Sorrento till he was nine, and then he was boarded with a worthy man, who superintended his education and taught him music. From his earliest childhood he has known me as his sister, and you cannot think how happy I was when I saw him growing so like you. I have always considered him as a sure pledge of our final union. I was ever thinking what would happen when we met, for I knew that he would have the same influence over you as he has over me. I was sure you would marry me and make him legitimate."

"And you have rendered all this, which would have made me happy, an impossibility."

"The fates decided so; we will say no more about it. On the death of the duke I left Naples, leaving Cesarino at the same boarding school, under the protection of the Prince de la Riccia, who has always looked upon him as a brother. Your son, though he does not know it, possesses the sum of twenty thousand ducats, of which I receive the interest, but you may imagine that I let him want for nothing. My only regret is that I cannot tell him I am his mother, as I think he would love me still more if he knew that he owed his being to me. You cannot think how glad I was to see your surprise to-day, and how soon you got to love him."

"He is wonderfully like me."

"That delights me. People must think that you were my mother's lover. My husband thinks that our friendship is due to the connection between you and my mother. He told me yesterday that Cesarino might be my brother on the mother's side, but not on my father's; as he had seen his father in the theatre, but that he could not possibly be my father, too. If I have children by Palesi all I have will go to them, but if not Cesarino will be my heir. My property is well secured, even if the Prince de Riccia were to die."

"Come," said she, drawing me in the direction of her bed-room. She opened a large box which contained her jewels and diamonds, and shares to the amount of fifty thousand ducats. Besides that she had a large amount of plate, and her talents which assured her the first place in all the Italian theatres.

"Do you know whether our dear Cesarino has been in love yet?" said I.

"I don't think so, but I fancy my pretty maid is in love with him. I shall keep my eyes open."

"You mustn't be too strict."

"No, but it isn't a good thing for a young man to engage too soon in that pleasure which makes one neglect everything else."

"Let me have him, I will teach him how to live."

"Ask all, but leave me my son. You must know that I never kiss him for fear of my giving way to excessive emotion. I wish you knew how good and pure he is, and how well he loves me, I could not refuse him anything."

"What will people say in Venice when they see Casanova again, who escaped from The Leads and has become twenty years younger?"

"You are going to Venice, then, for the Ascensa?"

"Yes, and you are going to Rome?"

"And to Naples, to see my friend the Duke de Matalone."

"I know him well. He has already had a son by the daughter of the Duke de Bovino, whom he married. She must be a charming woman to have made a man of him, for all Naples knew that he was impotent."

"Probably, she only knew the secret of making him a father."

"Well, it is possible."

We spent the time by talking with interest on various topics till Cesarino and the husband came back. The dear child finished his conquest of me at supper; he had a merry random wit, and all the Neapolitan vivacity. He sat down at the clavier, and after playing several pieces with the utmost skill he began to sing Neapolitan songs which made us all laugh. Therese only looked at him and me, but now and again she embraced her husband, saying, that in love alone lies happiness.

I thought then, and I think now, that this day was one of the happiest I have ever spent.

CHAPTER VII

The Corticelli—The Jew Manager Beaten—The False Charles Ivanoff and the Trick He Played Me—I Am Ordered to Leave Tuscany—I Arrive at Rome—My Brother Jean

At nine o'clock the next morning, the Abbe Gama was announced. The first thing he did was to shed tears of joy (as he said) at seeing me so well and prosperous after so many years. The reader will guess that the abbe addressed me in the most flattering terms, and perhaps he may know that one may be clever, experienced in the ways of the world, and even distrustful of flattery, but yet one's self-love, ever on the watch, listens to the flatterer, and thinks him pleasant. This polite and pleasant abbe, who had become extremely crafty from having lived all his days amongst the high dignitaries at the court of the 'Servus Servorum Dei' (the best school of strategy), was not altogether an ill-disposed man, but both his disposition and his profession conspired to make him inquisitive; in fine, such as I have depicted him in the first volume of these Memoirs. He wanted to hear my adventures, and did not wait for me to ask him to tell his story. He told me at great length the various incidents in his life for the seventeen years in which we had not seen one another. He had left the service of the King of Spain for that of the King of Portugal, he was secretary of embassy to the Commander Almada, and he had been obliged to leave Rome because the Pope Rezzonico would not allow the King of Portugal to punish certain worthy Jesuit assassins, who had only broken his arm as it happened, but who had none the less meant to take his life. Thus, Gama was staying in Italy corresponding with Almada and the famous Carvalho, waiting for the dispute to be finished before he returned to Rome. In point of fact this was the only substantial incident in the abbe's story, but he worked in so many episodes of no consequence that it lasted for an hour. No doubt he wished me to shew my gratitude by telling him all my adventures without reserve; but the upshot of it was that we both shewed ourselves true diplomatists, he in lengthening his story, I in shortening mine, while I could not help feeling some enjoyment in baulking the curiosity of my cassocked friend.

"What are you going to do in Rome?" said he, indifferently.

"I am going to beg the Pope to use his influence in my favour with the State Inquisitors at Venice."

It was not the truth, but one lie is as good as another, and if I had said I was only going for amusement's sake he would not have believed me. To tell the truth to an unbelieving man is to prostitute, to murder it. He then begged me to enter into a correspondence with him, and as that bound me to nothing I agreed to do so.

"I can give you a mark of my friendship," said he, "by introducing you to the Marquis de Botta-Adamo, Governor of Tuscany; he is supposed to be a friend of the regent's."

I accepted his offer gratefully, and he began to sound me about Therese, but found my lips as tightly closed as the lid of a miser's coffer. I told him she was a child when I made the acquaintance of her family at Bologna, and that the resemblance between her brother and myself was a mere accident—a freak of nature. He happened to catch sight of a well-written manuscript on the table, and asked me if that superb writing was my secretary's. Costa, who was present, answered in Spanish that he wrote it. Gama overwhelmed him with compliments, and begged me to send Costa to him to copy some letters. I guessed that he wanted to pump him about me, and said that I needed his services all the day.

"Well, well," said the abbe, "another time will do." I gave him no answer. Such is the character of the curious.

I am not referring to that curiosity which depends on the occult sciences, and endeavours to pry into the future—the daughter of ignorance and superstition, its victims are either foolish or ignorant. But the Abbe Gama was neither; he was naturally curious, and his employment made him still more so, for he was paid to find out everything. He was a diplomatist; if he had been a little lower down in the social scale he would have been treated as a spy.

He left me to pay some calls, promising to be back by dinner-time.

Dr. Vannini brought me another servant, of the same height as the first, and engaged that he should obey orders and guess nothing. I thanked the academician and inn-keeper, and ordered him to get me a sumptuous dinner.

The Corticelli was the first to arrive, bringing with her her brother, an effeminate-looking young man, who played the violin moderately well, and her mother, who informed me that she never allowed her daughter to dine out without herself and her son.

"Then you can take her back again this instant," said I, "or take this ducat to dine somewhere else, as I don't want your company or your son's."

She took the ducat, saying that she was sure she was leaving her daughter in good hands.

"You may be sure of that," said I, "so be off."

The daughter made such witty observations on the above dialogue that I could not help laughing, and I began to be in love with her. She was only thirteen, and was so small that she looked ten. She was well-made, lively, witty, and fairer than is usual with Italian women, but to this day I cannot conceive how I fell in love with her.

The young wanton begged me to protect her against the manager of the opera, who was a Jew. In the agreement she had made with him he had engaged to let her dance a 'pas de deux' in the second opera, and he had not kept his word. She begged me to compel the Jew to fulfil his engagement, and I promised to do so.

The next guest was Redegonde, who came from Parma. She was a tall, handsome woman, and Costa told me she was the sister of my new footman. After I had talked with her for two or three minutes I found her remarks well worthy of attention.

Then came the Abbe Gama, who congratulated me on being seated between two pretty girls. I made him take my place, and he began to entertain them as if to the manner born; and though the girls were laughing at him, he was not in the least disconcerted. He thought he was amusing them, and on watching his expression I saw that his self-esteem prevented him seeing that he was making a fool of himself; but I did not guess that I might make the same mistake at his age.

Wretched is the old man who will not recognize his old age; wretched unless he learn that the sex whom he seduced so often when he was young will despise him now if he still attempts to gain their favour.

My fair Therese, with her husband and my son, was the last to arrive. I kissed Therese and then my son, and sat down between them, whispering to Therese that such a dear mysterious trinity must not be parted; at which Therese smiled sweetly. The abbe sat down between Redegonde and the Corticelli, and amused us all the time by his agreeable conversation.

I laughed internally when I observed how respectfully my new footman changed his sister's plate, who appeared vain of honours to which her brother could lay no claim. She was not kind; she whispered to me, so that he could not hear,—

"He is a good fellow, but unfortunately he is rather stupid."

I had put in my pocket a superb gold snuff-box, richly enamelled and adorned with a perfect likeness of myself. I had had it made at Paris, with the intention of giving it to Madame d'Urfe, and I had not done so because the painter had made me too young. I had filled it with some excellent Havana snuff which M. de Chavigny had given me, and of which Therese was very fond; I was waiting for her to ask me for a pinch before I drew it out of my pocket.

The Abbe Gama, who had some exceedingly good snuff in an Origonela box, sent a pinch to Therese, and she sent him her snuff in a tortoise-shell box encrusted with gold in arabesques—an exquisite piece of workmanship. Gama criticised Therese's snuff, while I said that I found it delicious but that I thought I had some better myself. I took out my snuff-box, and opening it offered her a pinch. She did not notice the portrait, but she agreed that my snuff was vastly superior to hers.

"Well, would you like to make an exchange?" said I. "Certainly, give me some paper."

"That is not requisite; we will exchange the snuff and the snuff-boxes."

So saying, I put Therese's box in my pocket and gave her mine shut. When she saw the portrait, she gave a cry which puzzled everybody, and her first motion was to kiss the portrait.

"Look," said she to Cesarino, "here is your portrait."

Cesarino looked at it in astonishment, and the box passed from hand to hand. Everybody said that it was my portrait, taken ten years ago, and that it might pass for a likeness of Cesarino. Therese got quite excited, and swearing that she would never let the box out of her hands again, she went up to her son and kissed him several times. While this was going on I watched the Abbe

Gama, and I could see that he was making internal comments of his own on this affecting scene.

The worthy abbe went away towards the evening, telling me that he would expect me to breakfast next morning.

I spent the rest of the day in making love to Redegonde, and Therese, who saw that I was pleased with the girl, advised me to declare myself, and promised that she would ask her to the house as often as I liked. But Therese did not know her.

Next morning Gama told me that he had informed Marshal Botta that I would come and see him, and he would present me at four o'clock. Then the worthy abbe, always the slave of his curiosity, reproached me in a friendly manner for not having told him anything about my fortune.

"I did not think it was worth mentioning, but as you are interested in the subject I may tell you that my means are small, but that I have friends whose purses are always open to me."

"If you have true friends you are a rich man, but true friends are scarce."

I left the Abbe Gama, my head full of Redegonde, whom I preferred to the young Corticelli, and I went to pay her a visit; but what a reception! She received me in a room in which were present her mother, her uncle, and three or four dirty, untidy little monkeys: these were her brothers.'

"Haven't you a better room to receive your friends in?" said I.

"I have no friends, so I don't want a room."

"Get it, my dear, and you will find the friends come fast enough. This is all very well for you to welcome your relations in, but not persons like myself who come to do homage to your charms and your talents."

"Sir," said the mother, "my daughter has but few talents, and thinks nothing of her charms, which are small."

"You are extremely modest, and I appreciate your feelings; but everybody does not see your daughter with the same eyes, and she pleased me greatly."

"That is an honour for her, and we are duly sensible of it, but not so as to be over-proud. My daughter will see you as often as you please, but here, and in no other place."

"But I am afraid of being in the way here."

"An honest man is never in the way."

I felt ashamed, for nothing so confounds a libertine as modesty in the mouth of poverty; and not knowing what to answer I took my leave.

I told Therese of my unfortunate visit, and we both, laughed at it; it was the best thing we could do.

"I shall be glad to see you at the opera," said she, "and you can get into my dressing-room if you give the door-keeper a small piece of money."

The Abbe Gama came as he promised, to take me to Marshal Botta, a man of high talents whom the affair of Genoa had already rendered famous. He was in command of the Austrian army when the people, growing angry at the sight of the foreigners, who had only come to put them under the Austrian yoke, rose in revolt and made them leave the town. This patriotic riot saved the Republic. I found him in the midst of a crowd of ladies and gentlemen, whom he left to welcome me. He talked about Venice in a way that shewed he understood the country thoroughly, and I conversed to him on France, and, I believe, satisfied him. In his turn he spoke of the Court of Russia, at which he was staying when Elizabeth Petrovna, who was still reigning at the period in question, so easily mounted the throne of her father, Peter the Great. "It is only in Russia," said he, "that poison enters into politics."

At the time when the opera began the marshal left the room, and everybody went away. On my way the abbe assured me, as a matter of course, that I had pleased the governor, and I afterwards went to the theatre, and obtained admission to Therese's dressing-room for a tester. I found her in the hands of her pretty chamber-maid, and she advised me to go to Redegonde's dressing-room, as she played a man's part, and might, perhaps, allow me to assist in her toilette.

I followed her advice, but the mother would not let me come in, as her daughter was just going to dress. I assured her that I would turn my back all the time she was dressing, and on this condition she let me in, and made me sit down at a table on which stood a mirror, which enabled me to see all Redegonde's most secret parts to advantage; above all, when she lifted her legs to put on her breeches, either most awkwardly or most cleverly, according to her intentions. She did not lose anything by what she shewed, however, for I was so pleased, that to possess her charms I would have signed any conditions she cared to impose upon me.

"Redegonde must know," I said to myself, "that I could see everything in the glass;" and the idea inflamed me. I did not turn round till the mother gave me leave, and I then admired my charmer as a young man of five feet one, whose shape left nothing to be desired.

Redegonde went out, and I followed her to the wings.

"My dear," said I, "I am going to talk plainly to you. You have inflamed my passions and I shall die if you do not make me happy."

"You do not say that you will die if you chance to make me unhappy."

"I could not say so, because I cannot conceive such a thing as possible. Do not trifle with me, dear Redegonde, you must be aware that I saw all in the mirror, and I cannot think that you are so cruel as to arouse my passions and then leave me to despair."

"What could you have seen? I don't know what you are talking about."

"May be, but know that I have seen all your charms. What shall I do to possess you?"

"To possess me? I don't understand you, sir; I'm an honest girl."

"I dare say; but you wouldn't be any less honest after making me happy. Dear Redegonde, do not let me languish for you, but tell me my fate now this instant."

"I do not know what to tell you, but you can come and see me whenever you like."

"When shall I find you alone?"

"Alone! I am never alone."

"Well, well, that's of no consequence; if only your mother is present, that comes to the same thing. If she is sensible, she will pretend not to see anything, and I will give you a hundred ducats each time."

"You are either a madman, or you do not know what sort of people we are."

With these words she went on, and I proceeded to tell Therese what had passed.

"Begin," said she, "by offering the hundred ducats to the mother, and if she refuses, have no more to do with them, and go elsewhere."

I returned to the dressing-room, where I found the mother alone, and without any ceremony spoke as follows:—

"Good evening, madam, I am a stranger here; I am only staying a week, and I am in love with your daughter. If you like to be obliging, bring her to sup with me. I will give you a hundred sequins each time, so you see my purse is in your power."

"Whom do you think you are talking to, sir? I am astonished at your impudence. Ask the townsfolk what sort of character I bear, and whether my daughter is an honest girl or not! and you will not make such proposals again."

"Good-bye, madam."

"Good-bye, sir."

As I went out I met Redegonde, and I told her word for word the conversation I had had with her mother. She burst out laughing.

"Have I done well or ill?" said I.

"Well enough, but if you love me come and see me."

"See you after what your mother said?"

"Well, why not, who knows of it?"

"Who knows? You don't know me, Redegonde. I do not care to indulge myself in idle hopes, and I thought I had spoken to you plainly enough."

Feeling angry, and vowing to have no more to do with this strange girl, I supped with Therese, and spent three delightful hours with her. I had a great deal of writing to do the next day and kept in doors, and in the evening I had a visit from the young Corticelli, her mother and brother. She begged me to keep my promise regarding the manager of the theatre, who would not let her dance the 'pas de deux' stipulated for in the agreement.

"Come and breakfast with me to-morrow morning," said I, "and I will speak to the Israelite in your presence—at least I will do so if he comes."

"I love you very much," said the young wanton, "can't I stop a little longer here."

"You may stop as long as you like, but as I have got some letters to finish, I must ask you to excuse my entertaining you."

"Oh! just as you please."

I told Costa to give her some supper.

I finished my letters and felt inclined for a little amusement, so I made the girl sit by me and proceeded to toy with her, but in such a way that her mother could make no objection. All at once the brother came up and tried to join in the sport, much to my astonishment.

"Get along with you," said I, "you are not a girl."

At this the young scoundrel proceeded to shew me his sex, but in such an indecent fashion that his sister, who was sitting on my knee, burst out laughing and took refuge with her mother, who was sitting at the other end of the room in gratitude for the good supper I had given her. I rose from my chair, and after giving the impudent pederast a box on the ear I asked the mother with what intentions she had brought the young rascal to my house. By way of reply the infamous woman said,—

"He's a pretty lad, isn't he?"

I gave him a ducat for the blow I had given him, and told the mother to begone, as she disgusted me. The pathic took my ducat, kissed my hand, and they all departed.

I went to bed feeling amused at the incident, and wondering at the wickedness of a mother who would prostitute her own son to the basest of vices.

Next morning I sent and asked the Jew to call on me. The Corticelli came with her mother, and the Jew soon after, just as we were going to breakfast.

I proceeded to explain the grievance of the young dancer, and I read the agreement he had made with her, telling him politely that I could easily force him to fulfil it. The Jew put in several excuses, of which the Corticelli demonstrated the futility. At last the son of Judah was forced to give in, and promised to speak to the ballet-master the same day, in order that she might dance the 'pas' with the actor she named.

"And that, I hope, will please your excellency," he added, with a low bow, which is not often a proof of sincerity, especially among Jews.

When my guests had taken leave I went to the Abbe Gama, to dine with Marshal Botta who had asked us to dinner. I made the acquaintance there of Sir Mann, the English ambassador, who was the idol of Florence, very rich, of the most pleasing manners although an Englishman; full of wit, taste, and a great lover of the fine arts. He invited me to come next day and see his house and garden. In this home he had made—furniture, pictures, choice books—all shewed the man of genius. He called on me, asked me to dinner, and had the politeness to include Therese, her husband, and Cesarino in the invitation. After dinner my son sat down at the clavier and delighted the company by his exquisite playing. While we were talking of likenesses, Sir Mann shewed us some miniatures of great beauty.

Before leaving, Therese told me that she had been thinking seriously of me.

"In what respect?" I asked.

"I have told Redegonde that I am going to call for her, that I will keep her to supper, and have her taken home. You must see that this last condition is properly carried out. Come to supper too, and have your carriage in waiting. I leave the rest to you. You will only be a few minutes with her, but that's something; and the first step leads far."

"An excellent plan. I will sup with you, and my carriage shall be ready.
I will tell you all about it to-morrow."

I went to the house at nine o'clock, and was welcomed as an unexpected guest. I told Redegonde that I was glad to meet her, and she replied that she had not hoped to have the pleasure of seeing me. Redegonde was the only one who had any appetite; she ate capitally, and laughed merrily at the stories I told her.

After supper Therese asked her if she would like to have a sedan-chair sent for, or if she would prefer to be taken back in my carriage.

"If the gentleman will be so kind," said she, "I need not send for a chair."

I thought this reply of such favourable omen that I no longer doubted of my success. After she had wished the others good night, she took my arm, pressing it as she did so; we went down the stairs, and she got into the carriage. I got in after her, and on attempting to sit down I found the place taken.

"Who is that?" I cried.

Redegonde burst out laughing, and informed me it was her mother.

I was done; I could not summon up courage to pass it off as a jest. Such a shock makes a man stupid; for a moment it numbs all the mental faculties, and wounded self-esteem only gives place to anger.

I sat down on the front seat and coldly asked the mother why she had not come up to supper with us. When the carriage stopped at their door, she asked me to come in, but I told her I would rather not. I felt that for a little more I would have boxed her ears, and the man at the house door looked very like a cut-throat.

I felt enraged and excited physically as well as mentally, and though I had never been to see the Corticelli, told the coachman to drive there immediately, as I felt sure of finding her well disposed.

Everybody was gone to bed. I knocked at the door till I got an answer, I gave my name, and I was let in, everything being in total darkness. The mother told me she would light a candle, and that if she had expected me she would have waited up in spite of the cold. I felt as if I were in the middle of an iceberg. I heard the girl laughing, and going up to the bed and passing my hand over it I came across some plain tokens of the masculine gender. I had got hold of her brother. In the meanwhile the mother had got a candle, and I saw the girl with the bedclothes up to her chin, for, like her brother, she was as naked as my hand. Although no Puritan, I was shocked.

"Why do you allow this horrible union?" I said to the mother.

"What harm is there? They are brother and sister."

"That's just what makes it a criminal matter."

"Everything is perfectly innocent."

"Possibly; but it's not a good plan."

The pathic escaped from the bed and crept into his mother's, while the little wanton told me there was really no harm, as they only loved each other as brother and sister, and that if I wanted her to sleep by herself all I had to do was to get her a new bed. This speech, delivered with arch simplicity, in her Bolognese jargon, made me laugh with all my heart, for in the violence of her gesticulations she had disclosed half her charms, and I saw nothing worth looking at. In spite of that, it was doubtless decreed that I should fall in love with her skin, for that was all she had.

If I had been alone I should have brought matters to a crisis on the spot, but I had a distaste to the presence of her mother and her scoundrelly brother. I was afraid lest some unpleasant scenes might follow. I gave her ten ducats to buy a bed, said good night, and left the house. I returned to my lodging, cursing the too scrupulous mothers of the opera girls.

I passed the whole of the next morning with Sir Mann, in his gallery, which contained some exquisite paintings, sculptures, mosaics, and engraved gems. On leaving him, I called on Therese and informed her of my misadventure of the night before. She laughed heartily at my story, and I laughed too, in spite of a feeling of anger due to my wounded self-esteem.

"You must console yourself," said she; "you will not find much difficulty in filling the place in your affections."

"Ah! why are you married?"

"Well, it's done; and there's no helping it. But listen to me. As you can't do without someone, take up with the Corticelli; she's as good as any other woman, and won't keep you waiting long."

On my return to my lodging, I found the Abbe Gama, whom I had invited to dinner, and he asked me if I would accept a post to represent Portugal at the approaching European Congress at Augsburg. He told me that if I did the work well, I could get anything I liked at Lisbon.

"I am ready to do my best," said I; "you have only to write to me, and I will tell you where to direct your letters." This proposal made me long to become a diplomatist.

In the evening I went to the opera-house and spoke to the ballet-master, the dancer who was to take part in the 'pas de deux', and to the Jew, who told me that my protegee should be satisfied in two or three days, and that she should perform her favourite 'pas' for the rest of the carnival. I saw the Corticelli, who told me she had got her bed, and asked me to come to supper. I accepted the invitation, and when the opera was over I went to her house.

Her mother, feeling sure that I would pay the bill, had ordered an excellent supper for four, and several flasks of the best Florence wine. Besides that, she gave me a bottle of the wine called Oleatico, which I found excellent. The three Corticellis unaccustomed to good fare and wine, ate like a troop, and began to get intoxicated. The mother and son went to bed without ceremony, and the little wanton invited me to follow their example. I should have liked to do so, but I did not dare. It was very cold and there was no fire in the room, there was only one blanket on the bed, and I might have caught a bad cold, and I was too fond of my good health to expose myself to such a danger. I therefore satisfied myself by taking her on my knee, and after a few preliminaries she abandoned herself to my transports, endeavouring to persuade me that I had got her maidenhead. I pretended to believe her, though I cared very little whether it were so or not.

I left her after I had repeated the dose three or four times, and gave her fifty sequins, telling her to get a good wadded coverlet and a large brazier, as I wanted to sleep with her the next night.

Next morning I received an extremely interesting letter from Grenoble. M. de Valenglard informed me that the fair Mdlle. Roman, feeling convinced that her horoscope would never come true unless she went to Paris, had gone to the capital with her aunt.

Her destiny was a strange one; it depended on the liking I had taken to her and my aversion to marriage, for it lay in my power to have married the handsomest woman in France, and in that case it is not likely that she would have become the mistress of Louis XV. What strange whim could have made me indicate in her horoscope the necessity of her journeying to Paris; for even if there were such a science as astrology I was no astrologer; in fine, her destiny depended on my absurd fancy. And in history, what a number of extraordinary events would never have happened if they had not been predicted!

In the evening I went to the theatre, and found my Corticelli clad in a pretty cloak, while the other girls looked at me contemptuously, for they were enraged at the place being taken; while the proud favourite caressed me with an air of triumph which became her to admiration.

In the evening I found a good supper awaiting me, a large brazier on the hearth, and a warm coverlet on the bed. The mother shewed me all the things her daughter had bought, and complained that she had not got any clothes for her brother. I made her happy by giving her a few louis.

When I went to bed I did not find my mistress in any amorous transports, but in a wanton and merry mood. She made me laugh, and as she let me do as I liked I was satisfied. I gave her a watch when I left her, and promised to sup with her on the following night. She was to have danced the pas de deux, and I went to see her do it, but to my astonishment she only danced with the other girls.

When I went to supper I found her in despair. She wept and said that I must avenge her on the Jew, who had excused himself by putting the fault on somebody else, but that he was a liar. I promised everything to quiet her, and after spending several hours in her company I returned home, determined to give the Jew a bad quarter of an hour. Next morning I sent Costa to ask him to call on me, but the rascal sent back word that he was not coming, and if the Corticelli did not like his theatre she might try another.

I was indignant, but I knew that I must dissemble, so I only laughed. Nevertheless, I had pronounced his doom, for an Italian never forgets to avenge himself on his enemy; he knows it is the pleasure of the gods.

As soon as Costa had left the room, I called Le Duc and told him the story, saying that if I did not take vengeance I should be dishonoured, and that it was only he who could procure the scoundrel a good thrashing for daring to insult me.

"But you know, Le Duc, the affair must be kept secret."

"I only want twenty-four hours to give you an answer."

I knew what he meant, and I was satisfied.

Next morning Le Duc told me he had spent the previous day in learning the Jew's abode and habits, without asking anybody any questions.

"To-day I will not let him go out of my sight. I shall find out at what hour he returns home, and to-morrow you shall know the results."

"Be discreet," said I, "and don't let anybody into your plans."

"Not I!"

Next day, he told me that if the Jew came home at the same time and by the same way as before, he would have a thrashing before he got to bed.

"Whom have you chosen for this expedition?"

"Myself. These affairs ought to be kept secret, and a secret oughtn't to be known to more than two people. I am sure that everything will turn out well, but when you are satisfied that the ass's hide has been well tanned, will there be anything to be picked up?"

"Twenty-five sequins."

"That will do nicely. When I have done the trick I shall put on my great coat again and return by the back door. If necessary Costa himself will be able to swear that I did not leave the house, and that therefore I cannot have committed the assault. However, I shall put my pistols in my pocket in case of accidents, and if anybody tries to arrest me I shall know how to defend myself."

Next morning he came coolly into my room while Costa was putting on my dressing-gown, and when we were alone he said,—

"The thing's done. Instead of the Jew's running away when he received the first blow he threw himself on to the ground. Then I tanned his skin for him nicely, but on hearing some people coming up I ran off. I don't know whether I did for him, but I gave him two sturdy blows on the head. I should be sorry if he were killed, as then he could not see about the dance."

This jest did not arouse my mirth; the matter promised to be too serious.

Therese had asked me to dine with the Abbe Gama and M. Sassi, a worthy man, if one may prostitute the name of man to describe a being whom cruelty has separated from the rest of humanity; he was the first castrato of the opera. Of course the Jew's mishap was discussed.

"I am sorry for him," said I, "though he is a rascally fellow."

"I am not at all sorry for him myself," said Sassi, "he's a knave."

"I daresay that everybody will be putting down his wooden baptism to my account."

"No," said the abbe, "people say that M. Casanova did the deed for good reasons of his own."

"It will be difficult to pitch on the right man," I answered, "the rascal has pushed so many worthy people to extremities that he must have a great many thrashings owing him."

The conversation then passed to other topics, and we had a very pleasant dinner.

In a few days the Jew left his bed with a large plaster on his nose, and although I was generally regarded as the author of his misfortune the matter was gradually allowed to drop, as there were only vague suspicions to go upon. But the Corticelli, in an ecstasy of joy, was stupid enough to talk as if she were sure it was I who had avenged her, and she got into a rage when I would not admit the deed; but, as may be guessed, I was not foolish enough to do so, as her imprudence might have been a hanging matter for me.

I was well enough amused at Florence, and had no thoughts of leaving, when one day Vannini gave me a letter which someone had left for me. I opened it in his presence, and found it contained a bill of exchange for two hundred Florentine crowns on Sasso Sassi. Vannini looked at it and told me it was a good one. I went into my room to read the letter, and I was astonished to find it signed "Charles Ivanoff." He dated it from Pistoia, and told me that in his poverty and misfortune he had appealed to an Englishman who was leaving Florence for Lucca, and had generously given him a bill of exchange for two hundred crowns, which he had written in his presence. It was made payable to bearer.

"I daren't cash it in Florence," said he, "as I am afraid of being arrested for my unfortunate affair at Genoa. I entreat you, then, to have pity on me, to get the bill cashed, and to bring me the money here, that I may pay my landlord and go."

It looked like a very simple matter, but I might get into trouble, for the note might be forged; and even if it were not I should be declaring myself a friend or a correspondent, at all events, of a man who had been posted. In this dilemma I took the part of taking the bill of exchange to him in person. I went to the posting establishment, hired two horses, and drove to Pistoia. The landlord himself took me to the rascal's room, and left me alone with him.

I did not stay more than three minutes, and all I said was that as Sassi knew me I did not wish him to think that there was any kind of connection between us.

"I advise you," I said, "to give the bill to your landlord, who will cash it at M. Sassi's and bring you your change."

"I will follow your advice," he said, and I therewith returned to Florence.

I thought no more of it, but in two days' time I received a visit from M. Sassi and the landlord of the inn at Pistoia. The banker shewed me the bill of exchange, and said that the person who had given it me had deceived me, as it was not in the writing of the Englishman whose name it bore, and that even if it were, the Englishman not having any money with Sassi could not draw a bill of exchange.

"The inn-keeper here," said he, "discounted the bill, the Russian has gone off, and when I told him that it was a forgery he said that he knew Charles Ivanoff had it of you, and that thus he had made no difficulty in cashing it; but now he wants you to return him two hundred crowns."

"Then he will be disappointed!"

I told all the circumstances of the affair to Sassi; I shewed him the rascal's letter; I made Dr. Vannini, who had given it me, come up, and he said he was ready to swear that he had seen me take the bill of exchange out of the letter, that he had examined it, and had thought it good.

On this the banker told the inn-keeper that he had no business to ask me to pay him the money; but he persisted in his demand, and dared to say that I was an accomplice of the Russian's.

In my indignation I ran for my cane, but the banker held me by the arm, and the impertinent fellow made his escape without a thrashing.

"You had a right to be angry," said M. Sassi, "but you must not take any notice of what the poor fellow says in his blind rage."

He shook me by the hand and went out.

Next day the chief of police, called the auditor at Florence, sent me a note begging me to call on him. There was no room for hesitation, for as a stranger I felt that I might look on this invitation as an intimation. He received me very politely, but he said I should have to repay the landlord his two hundred crowns, as he would not have discounted the bill if he had not seen me bring it. I replied that as a judge he could not condemn me unless he thought me the Russian's accomplice, but instead of answering he repeated that I would have to pay.

"Sir," I replied, "I will not pay."

He rang the bell and bowed, and I left him, walking towards the banker's, to whom I imparted the conversation I had had from the auditor. He was extremely astonished, and at my request called on him to try and make him listen to reason. As we parted I told him that I was dining with the Abbe Gama.

When I saw the abbe I told him what had happened, and he uttered a loud exclamation of astonishment.

"I foresee," he said, "that the auditor will not let go his hold, and if M. Sassi does not succeed with him I advise you to speak to Marshal
Botta."

"I don't think that will be necessary; the auditor can't force me to pay."

"He can do worse."

"What can he do?".

"He can make you leave Florence."

"Well, I shall be astonished if he uses his power in this case, but rather than pay I will leave the town. Let us go to the marshal."

We called on him at four o'clock, and we found the banker there, who had told him the whole story.

"I am sorry to tell you," said M. Sassi, "that I could do nothing with the auditor, and if you want to remain in Florence you will have to pay."

"I will leave as soon as I receive the order," said I; "and as soon as I reach another state I will print the history of this shameful perversion of justice."

"It's an incredible, a monstrous sentence," said the marshal, "and I am sorry I cannot interfere. You are quite right," he added, "to leave the place rather than pay."

Early the next morning a police official brought me a letter from the auditor, informing me that as he could not, from the nature of the case, oblige me to pay, he was forced to warn me to leave Florence in three days, and Tuscany in seven. This, he added, he did in virtue of his office; but whenever the Grand Duke, to whom I might appeal, had quashed his judgment I might return.

I took a piece of paper and wrote upon it, "Your judgment is an iniquitous one, but it shall be obeyed to the letter."

At that moment I gave orders to pack up and have all in readiness for my departure. I spent three days of respite in amusing myself with Therese. I also saw the worthy Sir Mann, and I promised the Corticelli to fetch her in Lent, and spend some time with her in Bologna. The Abbe Gama did not leave my side for three days, and shewed himself my true friend. It was a kind of triumph for me; on every side I heard regrets at my departure, and curses of the auditor. The Marquis Botta seemed to approve my conduct by giving me a dinner, the table being laid for thirty, and the company being composed of the most distinguished people in Florence. This was a delicate attention on his part, of which I was very sensible.

I consecrated the last day to Therese, but I could not find any opportunity to ask her for a last consoling embrace, which she would not have refused me under the circumstances, and which I should still fondly remember. We promised to write often to one another, and we embraced each other in a way to make her husband's heart ache. Next day I started on my journey, and got to Rome in thirty-six hours.

It was midnight when I passed under the Porta del Popolo, for one may enter the Eternal City at any time. I was then taken to the custom-house, which is always open, and my mails were examined. The only thing they are strict about at Rome is books, as if they feared the light. I had about thirty volumes, all more or less against the Papacy, religion, or the virtues inculcated thereby. I had resolved to surrender them without any dispute, as I felt tired and wanted to go to bed, but the clerk told me politely to count them and leave them in his charge for the night, and he would bring them to my hotel in the morning. I did so, and he kept his word. He was well enough pleased when he touched the two sequins with which I rewarded him.

I put up at the Ville de Paris, in the Piazza di Spagna. It is the best inn in the town. All the world, I found, was drowned in sleep, but when they let me in they asked me to wait on the ground floor while a fire was lighted in my room. All the seats were covered with dresses, petticoats, and chemises, and I heard a small feminine voice begging me to sit on her bed. I approached and saw a laughing mouth, and two black eyes shining like carbuncles.

"What splendid eyes!" said I, "let me kiss them."

By way of reply she hid her head under the coverlet, and I slid a hasty hand under the sheets; but finding her quite naked, I drew it back and begged pardon. She put out her head again, and I thought I read gratitude for my moderation in her eyes.

"Who are you, my angel?"

"I am Therese, the inn-keeper's daughter, and this is my sister." There was another girl beside her, whom I had not seen, as her head was under the bolster.

"How old are you?"

"Nearly seventeen."

"I hope I shall see you in my room to-morrow morning."

"Have you any ladies with you?"

"No."

"That's a pity, as we never go to the gentlemen's rooms."

"Lower the coverlet a little; I can't hear what you say."

"It's too cold."

"Dear Therese, your eyes make me feel as if I were in flames."

She put back her head at this, and I grew daring, and after sundry experiments I was more than ever charmed with her. I caressed her in a somewhat lively manner, and drew back my hand, again apologizing for my daring, and when she let me see her face I thought I saw delight rather than anger in her eyes and on her cheeks, and I felt hopeful with regard to her. I was just going to begin again, for I felt on fire; when a handsome chambermaid came to tell me that my room was ready and my fire lighted.

"Farewell till to-morrow," said I to Therese, but she only answered by turning on her side to go to sleep.

I went to bed after ordering dinner for one o'clock, and I slept till noon, dreaming of Therese. When I woke up, Costa told me that he had found out where my brother lived, and had left a note at the house. This was my brother Jean, then about thirty, and a pupil of the famous Raphael Mengs. This painter was then deprived of his pension on account of a war which obliged the King of Poland to live at Warsaw, as the Prussians occupied the whole electorate of Saxe. I had not seen my brother for ten years, and I kept our meeting as a holiday. I was sitting down to table when he came, and we embraced each other with transport. We spent an hour in telling, he his small adventures, and I my grand ones, and he told me that I should not stay at the hotel, which was too dear, but come and live at the Chevalier Mengs's house, which contained an empty room, where I could stay at a much cheaper rate.

"As to your table, there is a restaurant in the house where one can get a capital meal."

"Your advice is excellent," said I, "but I have not the courage to follow it, as I am in love with my landlord's daughter;" and I told him what had happened the night before.

"That's a mere nothing," said he, laughing; "you can cultivate her acquaintance without staying in the house."

I let myself be persuaded, and I promised to come to him the following day; and then we proceeded to take a walk about Rome.

I had many interesting memories of my last visit, and I wanted to renew my acquaintance with those who had interested me at that happy age when such impressions are so durable because they touch the heart rather than the mind; but I had to make up my mind to a good many disappointments, considering the space of time that had elapsed since I had been in Rome.

I went to the Minerva to find Donna Cecilia; she was no more in this world. I found out where her daughter Angelica lived, and I went to see her, but she gave me a poor reception, and said that she really scarcely remembered me.

"I can say the same," I replied, "for you are not the Angelica I used to know. Good-bye, madam!"

The lapse of time had not improved her personal appearance. I found out also where the printer's son, who had married Barbaruccia, lived, but—I put off the pleasure of seeing him till another time, and also my visit to the Reverend Father Georgi, who was a man of great repute in Rome. Gaspar Vivaldi had gone into the country.

My brother took me to Madame Cherubini. I found her mansion to be a splendid one, and the lady welcomed me in the Roman manner. I thought her pleasant and her daughters still more so, but I thought the crowd of lovers too large and too miscellaneous. There was too much luxury and ceremony, and the girls, one of whom was as fair as Love himself, were too polite to everybody. An interesting question was put to me, to which I answered in such a manner as to elicit another question, but to no purpose. I saw that the rank of my brother, who had introduced me, prevented my being thought a person of any consequence, and on hearing an abbe say, "He's Casanova's brother," I turned to him and said,—

"That's not correct; you should say Casanova's my brother."

"That comes to the same thing."

"Not at all, my dear abbe."

I said these words in a tone which commanded attention, and another abbe said,—

"The gentleman is quite right; it does not come to the same thing."

The first abbe made no reply to this. The one who had taken my part, and was my friend from that moment, was the famous

Winckelmann, who was unhappily assassinated at Trieste twelve years afterwards.

While I was talking to him, Cardinal Alexander Albani arrived. Winckelmann presented me to his eminence, who was nearly blind. He talked to me a great deal, without saying anything worth listening to. As soon as he heard that I was the Casanova who had escaped from The Leads, he said in a somewhat rude tone that he wondered I had the hardihood to come to Rome, where on the slightest hint from the State Inquisitors at Venice an 'ordine sanctissimo' would re-consign me to my prison. I was annoyed by this unseemly remark, and replied in a dignified voice,—

"It is not my hardihood in coming to Rome that your eminence should wonder at, but a man of any sense would wonder at the Inquisitors if they had the hardihood to issue an 'ordine sanctissimo' against me; for they would be perplexed to allege any crime in me as a pretext for thus infamously depriving me of my liberty."

This reply silenced his eminence. He was ashamed at having taken me for a fool, and to see that I thought him one. Shortly after I left and never set foot in that house again.

The Abbe Winckelmann went out with my brother and myself, and as he came with me to my hotel he did me the honour of staying to supper. Winckelmann was the second volume of the celebrated Abbe de Voisenon. He called for me next day, and we went to Villa Albani to see the Chevalier Mengs, who was then living there and painting a ceiling.

My landlord Roland (who knew my brother) paid me a visit at supper. Roland came from Avignon and was fond of good living. I told him I was sorry to be leaving him to stay with my brother, because I had fallen in love with his daughter Therese, although I had only spoken to her for a few minutes, and had only seen her head.

"You saw her in bed, I will bet!"

"Exactly, and I should very much like to see the rest of her. Would you be so kind as to ask her to step up for a few minutes?"

"With all my heart."

She came upstairs, seeming only too glad to obey her father's summons. She had a lithe, graceful figure, her eyes were of surpassing brilliancy, her features exquisite, her mouth charming; but taken altogether I did not like her so well as before. In return, my poor brother became enamoured of her to such an extent that he ended by becoming her slave. He married her next year, and two years afterwards he took her to Dresden. I saw her five years later with a pretty baby; but after ten years of married life she died of consumption.

I found Mengs at the Villa Albani; he was an indefatigable worker, and extremely original in his conceptions. He welcomed me, and said he was glad to be able to lodge me at his house in Rome, and that he hoped to return home himself in a few days, with his whole family.

I was astonished with the Villa Albani. It had been built by Cardinal Alexander, and had been wholly constructed from antique materials to satisfy the cardinal's love for classic art; not only the statues and the vases, but the columns, the pedestals—in fact, everything was Greek. He was a Greek himself, and had a perfect knowledge of antique work, and had contrived to spend comparatively little money compared with the masterpiece he had produced. If a sovereign monarch had had a villa like the cardinal's built, it would have cost him fifty million francs, but the cardinal made a much cheaper bargain.

As he could not get any ancient ceilings, he was obliged to have them painted, and Mengs was undoubtedly the greatest and the most laborious painter of his age. It is a great pity that death carried him off in the midst of his career, as otherwise he would have enriched the stores of art with numerous masterpieces. My brother never did anything to justify his title of pupil of this great artist. When I come to my visit to Spain in 1767, I shall have some more to say about Mengs.

As soon as I was settled with my brother I hired a carriage, a coachman, and a footman, whom I put into fancy livery, and I called on Monsignor Cornaro, auditor of the 'rota', with the intention of making my way into good society, but fearing lest he as a Venetian might get compromised, he introduced me to Cardinal Passionei, who spoke of me to the sovereign pontiff.

Before I pass on to anything else, I will inform my readers of what took place on the occasion of my second visit to this old cardinal, a great enemy of the Jesuits, a wit, and man of letters.

The End

www.ingramcontent.com/pod-product-compliance
Lightning Source LLC
Chambersburg PA
CBHW072317290526
45794CB00002B/689